Culture and Customs
of Panama

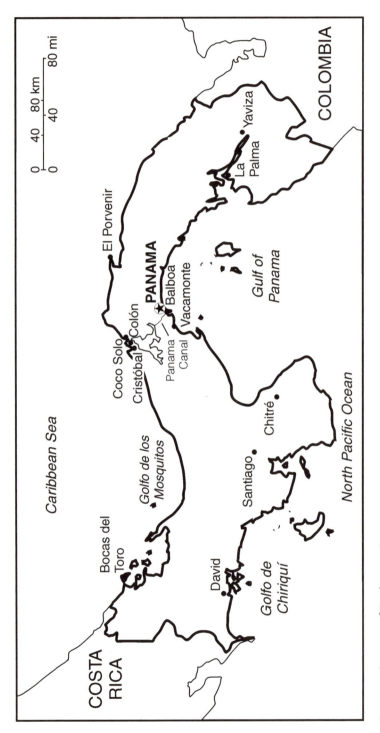

Panama. Courtesy of Bookcomp, Inc.

Culture and Customs of Panama

LA VERNE M. SEALES SOLEY

Culture and Customs of Latin America and the Caribbean
Peter Standish, Series Editor

GREENWOOD PRESS
Westport, Connecticut • London

Library of Congress Cataloging-in-Publication Data

Seales Soley, La Verne M.
   Culture and customs of Panama / La Verne M. Seales Soley.
   p.   cm.—(Culture and customs of Latin America and the Caribbean, ISSN 1521–8856)
   Includes bibliographical references and index.
   ISBN 978–0–313–33667–6 (alk. paper)
   1. Panama—Civilization.   2. Panama—Social life and customs.   I. Title.
   F1563.8.S44   2009
   306.097287—dc22   2008033531

British Library Cataloguing in Publication Data is available.

Library of Congress Catalog Card Number: 2008033531
ISBN: 978–0–313–33667–6
ISBN: 1521–8856

First published in 2009

Greenwood Press, 88 Post Road West, Westport, CT 06881
An imprint of Greenwood Publishing Group, Inc.
www.greenwood.com

Printed in the United States of America

Para mis tesoros: *Amir Abel and Lina Marie.* I dedicate this book to them, and their children, and their children's children. May they always remember the richness of their heritage

Contents

Series Foreword

CULTURE IS A problematic word. In everyday language, we tend to use it in at least two senses. On the one hand, we speak of cultured people and places full of culture—uses that imply a knowledge or presence of certain forms of behavior or of artistic expression that are socially prestigious. In this sense, large cities and prosperous people tend to be seen as the most cultured. On the other hand, there is an interpretation of culture that is broader and more anthropological; culture in this broader sense refers to whatever traditions, beliefs, customs, and creative activities characterize a given community—in short, it refers to what makes that community different from others. In this second sense, everyone has culture; indeed, it is impossible to be without culture. The problems associated with the idea of culture have been exacerbated in recent years by two trends: less respectful use of language and a greater blurring of cultural differences. Nowadays, culture often means little more than behavior, attitude, or atmosphere. We hear about the culture of the boardroom, of the football team, of the marketplace; there are books with titles like *The Culture of War* by Richard Gabriel (1990) or *The Culture of Narcissism* by Christopher Lasch (1979). In fact, as Christopher Clausen points out in an article published in the *American Scholar* (Summer 1996), we have gotten ourselves into trouble by using the term so sloppily.

People who study culture generally assume that culture (in the anthropological sense) is learned, not genetically determined. Another general assumption made in these days of multiculturalism has been that cultural differences should be respected rather than put under pressure to change. But these assumptions, too, have sometimes proved to be problematic. Multiculturalism is a fine ideal, but in practice it is not always easy to reconcile with the beliefs of the very people who advocate it—for example, is female circumcision an issue of human rights or just a different cultural practice?

The blurring of cultural differences is a process that began with the steamship, increased with radio, and is now racing ahead with the Internet. We are becoming globally homogenized. Since the English-speaking world (and the United States in particular) is the dominant force behind this process of homogenization, it behooves us to make efforts to understand the sensibilities of members of other cultures.

This series of books, a contribution toward that greater understanding, deals with the neighbors of the United States, with people who have just as much right to call themselves Americans. What are the historical, institutional, religious, and artistic features that make up the modern culture of peoples such as the Haitians, the Chileans, the Jamaicans, and the Guatemalans? How are their habits and assumptions different from our own? What can we learn from them? As we familiarize ourselves with the ways of other countries, we come to see our own from a new perspective.

Each volume in the series focuses on a single country. With slight variations to accommodate national differences, each begins by outlining the historical, political, ethnic, geographical, and linguistic context, as well as the religious and social customs, and then proceeds to a discussion of a variety of artistic activities, including the media, cinema, literature, and the visual and performing arts. The authors are all intimately acquainted with the countries concerned; some were born or brought up in them, and each has a professional commitment to enhancing the understanding of the culture in question. We are inclined to suppose that our ways of thinking and behaving are normal. And so they are . . . for us. We all need to realize that ours is only one culture among many, and that it is hard to establish by any rational criteria that ours as a whole is any better (or worse) than any other. As individual members of our immediate community, we know that we must learn to respect our differences from one another. Respect for differences between cultures is no less vital. This is particularly true of the United States, a nation of immigrants, but one that sometimes seems to be bent on destroying variety at home and, worse still, on having others follow suit. By learning about other people's cultures, we come to understand and respect them; we earn their respect for us; and, not least, we see ourselves in a new light.

Peter Standish
East Carolina University

Preface

WHEN MOST PEOPLE think of Panama, they immediately think of the Canal. But this Republic is much more than that; it is filled with history, culture, and diversity. From the colonial period to today, this book will try to explain how Panama came to be known, and continues to be known, as the "Crossroads of the World."

From colonial times, when it served as a base for Spanish conquistadors in the New World, to its present role as a strategic center of operations for the United States in Latin America, Panama's history has been forged in the shadow of other countries such as Spain, Colombia, and, more recently, the United States. The unique role within Latin America that Panama has played throughout history has been both a blessing and a burden for the citizens of this republic. The Canal has brought technology, economic growth, and a greater importance for Panama within the world. But along with these positive developments there have also been dictators, corruption, and a lack of true *soberanía* (sovereignty) for the country. After almost one hundred years, the Canal still has the ability to shape and influence the political and cultural climate of Panama.

The influence of the canal can be seen even among the people of Panama. With the Canal has come an influx of people from all parts of the world. These people have reestablished themselves within Panama and become part of the dense fabric of Panamanian culture. Among these people are Asians, Europeans, Africans, West Indians, and many Americans. With this mixture of people from around the world, it is not surprising that most Panamanians see their country as *Puente del Mundo, Corazón del Universo* (Bridge to the World, Heart of the Universe).

The people of Panama are as diverse as the nine provinces and five indigenous territories that make up the country. The climate of Panama is as varied as its people. With tropical rain forests in the south and eastern parts of the country and rainfall influencing the seasons more than the actual temperature change, Panama has one of the most extensive arrays of plant and wildlife within Central America.

The principle objective of *Culture and Customs of Panama* is to take the reader on a journey through these rich layers of history, culture, and geography, from Chiriquí in the north to Darién in the south, and to discover the essence of Panamanian life. Of specific interest to American readers is Panama's complex relationship to the United States. From its independence from Colombia in 1903, Panamanians have always felt the presence of the United States within their country. This constant presence has developed into a long-standing resentment of the United States by many Panamanian citizens, a resentment caused in part by the United States' construction and operation of the Canal as well as by the establishment of the Canal Zone. Not until the signing of the Torrijos-Carter Treaty in 1977 and the complete handing over of the Canal on December 31, 1999, did Panamanians feel a true sense of sovereignty within their country.

I have limited most of my discussions to Panama after its independence from Colombia, referencing its colonial history only to provide the context for the current state of the republic. While compiling the information for this book, I have also tried to limit my sources to include materials that are readily available to the native English speaker, allowing opportunities for further research on the part of the reader. I have, however, included some sources from Panama (such as schoolbooks, journals, newspaper articles, and magazines) in the Spanish language to allow for an accurate and balanced presentation of the facts.

As you read *Cultures and Customs of Panama*, I hope you will come to realize that more than just the Canal defines Panama. Panama is a country with a grand history and a highly individual role in the political and cultural theaters of Latin America.

Acknowledgments

I WOULD LIKE to thank my family, without whom this book would not have been possible.

I am indebted to my parents: my mother, Patricia Soley de Seales, who walked with me every step of the way, and my father, Herbert Evers Seales (1943–1991), whose belief in the value of education and knowledge has always guided me. My sister, Sharon Seales, and my brother, Herbert Evers Seales Jr. (Tito), have always been my greatest fans. I thank them for always believing in me and for giving me credit when I least expected but most needed it.

Loving thanks go to my husband Saley, a special gift in my life, for his understanding, for his unwavering support through this journey, and for helping me to believe even when I could not. My children Amir Abel and Lina Marie have been my continual source of inspiration. I am blessed to have them as my children.

I would also like to express my gratitude to Eric Stenclik for his support and encouragement, without which I would have not been able to finish this project. And finally many thanks to Kaitlin Ciarmiello for her professionalism and patience as she worked to see this project to completion.

Chronology

1501	Rodrigo de Bastidas, along with Juan de la Cosa and Vasco Núñez de Balboa, arrive in the Darién Region.
1502	Christopher Columbus visits Panama, and Santa María de Belén is founded.
1509	Diego de Nicuesa founds Nombre de Dios.
1510	Santa María La Antigua del Darién is founded.
1513	The Mar del Sur is discovered.
1519	Panama City is founded with Pedro Arias Ávila (or Pedrarias) as its governor.
1539	The beginning of the colonization period by the Spanish.
1671	Panama La Vieja is destroyed and Fuerte San Lorenzo is taken over by Henry Morgan.
1673	Panama City is rebuilt in its current location.
1749	The first university (San Javier) is founded in Panama by the Jesuits.
1821	Panama claims independence from Spain and voluntarily becomes part of *La Gran Colombia* (Union of Colombia, Venezuela, Ecuador, and Panama).

1826   Pan-Americanism Doctrine begins with an initiative by Simón Bolívar and the Panamanian Congress. Also formed at this time is the Organization of American States (OEA).

1830   *Gran Colombia* collapses, and Panama and Colombia become *Nueva Granada* (New Granada). First attempt by Panama to separate from *Nueva Granada*, led by José Domingo Espinar.

        First attempt by Panama to separate from *Nueva Granada*, led by José Domingo Espinar.

1831   Second attempt to separate from *Nueva Granada*, led by Juan Eligio Alzuru.

1840   Third attempt to separate from *Nueva Granada*, led by General Tomás Herrera.

1841   General Tomás Herrera creates the Isthmus Free State.

1846   The Mallarino-Bildack treaty between the United States and *Nueva Granada* gives the United States right to preferential transit through Panama.

1850   The Stephens-Paredes contract is signed in Bogota, Colombia, allowing a U.S. company to begin railroad construction across the Isthmus.

        The Panama Rail Company is created. Construction begins under George M. Totten.

1852   City of Colón founded as a result of a rail line connecting it to the rest of the Isthmus.

1855   Dr. Justo Arosemena creates the *Estado Federal del Istmo*, begins quest for Panama to be sovereign.

1878   Colombia cedes the interoceanic Universal Canal Company to Panama.

1880   Law is passed naming the last city of the railroad after Christopher Columbus.

1882   Excavations of the Canal by the French are started.

1891   Second attempt of Eligio Alzuru to separate from *Nueva Granada*.

1899–1902   The 1,000 Days War is started due to the constant struggles between conservatives and liberals.

1902   The United States intervenes in the war, and the Herran-Hay peace treaty is signed.

1903   On November 3, with the help of the United States, Panama declares its independence from Colombia, dissolving the union of *Nueva*

Granada. The Bunau-Varilla-Hay Treaty is signed, giving the United States the right to the perpetual use and occupation of the Canal Zone.

1904   First Panamanian constitution approved.

On February 20, Manual Amador Guerrero elected first president of the new Republic of Panama.

1905   Guardia-Pacheco declaration tries to solve disputes between Panama and Costa Rica.

1910   Anderson-Porras convention is signed between Costa Rica and Panama, ending border disputes.

1914   On August 15, the Panama Canal opens.

1921   Costa Rican forces invade Coto, and Panama responds.

1924   The Victoria-Vélez treaty is signed. Panama cedes Valley of Sixaola to Costa Rica, and the Jurado region to Colombia.

1925   36,000 hectares of land are given to the Tonosí Land Company, a subsidiary of the United Fruit Company.

1939   Panama is no longer a United States protectorate.

1968–1981   General Omar Torrijos overthrows elected president and becomes dictator.

1964   Anti United States public demonstrations and riots break out in the Panama Canal Zone, twenty two Panamanians and four soldiers died.

1977   General Omar Torrijos and United States President Jimmy Carter sign the Torrijos-Carter treaty where the United States promises to transfer control of the Canal to Panama December 31, 1999.

1981   General Omar Torrijos Herrera dies in a plane accident.

1983   Manuel Antonio Noriega promotes himself to General, becomes head of the National Guard and becomes the leader of Panama.

1988   The United States charges Noriega with drug trafficking.

1989   Panama is invaded by the United States, and Manuel Antonio Noriega is deposed.

1999   Mireya Moscoso becomes Panama's first female president. Complete transfer of the Panama Canal and total withdrawals off all military bases by the United States.

2004   Martín Torrijos Espino, the son of Omar Torrijos, wins the presidential election.

2006   Referendum to expand the Panama Canal approved.

2007   Project to expand the Panama Canal began and is projected to be completed 2014–2015.

2008   Irving Saladino wins Panama's first Gold Medal at the 2008 Summer Olympics in Beijing, China in the long jump competition.

1

Context

PANAMA'S GEOGRAPHIC LOCATION has dictated its role throughout history, deeply influencing its people, economy, government, and educational system. The Panama Canal has been the single most influential aspect of Panamanian life for more than one hundred years and still plays an important role in the country today.

LAND

The *República de Panamá* (Republic of Panama) is located in the southernmost part of Central America and connects Central America to the northwest of South America. Bordered on the east by Colombia and on the west by Costa Rica, Panama has 720 miles (1,160 kilometers) of coastline on the north and a 1,050-mile (1,690-kilometer) coastline on the south. These coasts are formed by the Caribbean Sea and the Pacific Ocean, respectively. The country extends for 480 miles (770 kilometers) from east to west, yet at its narrowest point it is only 30 miles wide. This makes the total area of Panama approximately 29,157 square miles (75,517 square kilometers).

The capital of the Republic of Panama is Panama City, located immediately to the east of the Panama Canal on the Pacific coastline. Panama City is a vibrant place with all the commodities you would expect to find in any modern city. The Panama Canal, which runs from north to south and divides the country, connects the Atlantic and Pacific Oceans.

Panama is divided into nine provinces (Bocas del Toro, Chiriquí, Coclé, Colón, Darién, Herrera, Los Santos, Panama, and Veraguas) and five indigenous territories (Embera, Kuna de Madugandí, Ngobe-Bugle, Kuna de Wargandí, and Kuna Yala). There are 67 districts or municipalities and 511 constituencies. The provinces of Panama and Colón make up the metropolitan region.

The temperature fluctuates between 80 and 90 degrees Fahrenheit (25–30 degrees Celsius), and the annual rainfall averages 51 to 118 inches (1.3–3 meters) per year depending on the region, giving Panama an almost yearlong tropical climate. The relative humidity often exceeds 80 percent. Panama has two seasons: the dry season, which extends from January to mid-April, and the rainy season, which runs from mid-April to December. In the summer season, between December and April, temperatures are slightly higher than the average yearlong temperature. During the rainy season, the average daily rainfall is one inch (28 millimeters).

At 11,401 feet in altitude (3,475 meters) the inactive Barú volcano in Chiriquí province is the highest peak in Panama. Two mountain ranges separate the country into natural regions: in the west, you can find the *Cordillera Central* (Tabasará Mountains) and in the east the *Cordillera de San Blas*. Panama's landscape can be described in terms of three distinct classifications: the highlands (elevations higher than 4,900 feet above sea level), temperate lands (2,300 to 4,900 feet), and lowlands, which make up more than 85 percent of Panama (below 2,300 feet).

Panama has more than 500 rivers. Among the longest are the Chagres and the Changuinola Rivers in the Caribbean basin, and the Chucunaque and the Tuira in the Pacific. Panama also has more than 1,600 islands; Isla Grande, Isla Taboga, and Las Islas de San Blas are among the most popular. At present, Panama's major environmental issues include land degradation, some deforestation, and water pollution from agricultural runoffs.

PEOPLE

Because of its location and history, Panama has a rather heterogeneous population. At the time of its colonization, Native American indigenous tribes such as the Chocó, Kuna, Guaymí/Chibcha, and other American Indian groups inhabited the region known today as Panama. After colonization, a *mestizo* (mixed Amerindian and European) population, of both American Indian and Spaniard heritage, emerged. After black slaves arrived with the Spanish conquistadors, other combinations of mixed races developed. In the nineteenth and twentieth centuries, the railroad projects, and later the construction of the Panama Canal, introduced successive waves of migrant and immigrant workers, including Chinese, French, Greeks, Italians, North American (mostly from the United States), and also blacks from the Caribbean Islands. As history unfolded, situations in other parts of the world also had an impact on immigration to the isthmus. For example, a wave of Lebanese citizens fleeing civil war in Lebanon and Indians came to the isthmus in search of better working opportunities, especially in the commercial sector, as did many Jews. In addition, many Chinese came for the construction of the railroad, and several others immigrated illegally during the period when Manuel Noriega was in power. Each ethnic group helped, in its own way, to shape the population and influence the culture of present-day Panama.

During and since the construction of the Panama Canal, people from the United States and West Indies, in particular, have had a significant influence on the country. The creation of the Canal Zone and the influx of West Indians, combined with the United States' segregation practices, forged a racially complex country. One of the most noticeable consequences was the resentment and class distinctions that erupted between blacks who came during colonization, the *Costeños* (people from the coast), and *Chombos*, a term used to refer to people of West Indian descent. West Indians were distinct from their black counterparts because of their use of English and their adherence to the Protestant faith. Although Panama has made efforts to integrate all racial groups into mainstream society, a small, dominant white class termed *Rabiblanco* (white tail) still shapes the country's economic and social life to a great extent.

Today, the majority of the population is *mestizo*. This ethnic group comprises approximately 70 percent of the country; an estimated 14 percent are blacks mostly of West Indian descent; whites account for about 10 percent and Native Americans about 6 percent.[1] Spanish is the official language. English is spoken by approximately 14 percent of the population;[2] speakers of English are primarily West Indians, their descendants, businesspeople, and professionals. English is spoken in tourist areas and in Colón and Panama City; however, as the tourism and banking industries continue to grow in Panama, so does the use of English. In Panama, one is able to hear many different languages that range from Urdu, Mandarin, Chinese, and Greek to several native Indian languages.

The *mestizo* population is found at all levels of society; nevertheless, the small group that comprises the upper class in the country (e.g., doctors, lawyers, successful business owners, engineers) is almost exclusively *mestizo*.

An estimated 14 percent of the population, blacks in Panama have faced discrimination from the time they arrived in the country.[3] Most of the West Indians who came to Panama were recruited to work on the Canal. They were first recruited by the French in Jamaica and later by the United States. The

United States began to enlist workers from other Caribbean islands after the Jamaican government prohibited further recruiting. This was due to the unsafe working conditions found in the area of the "big ditch," as the construction site of the Canal was sometimes called.

These West Indian workers were not only exploited but were also discriminated against. Their income was a fraction of what the recruited citizens of the United States were paid. Unlike the recruits from the islands, the United States citizens were offered great incentives and were encouraged to come to Panama to work on the "zone." These were very attractive offers, and they were paid for doing much less work. The jobs and working conditions for the American citizens were safer, and they had comforts that many could only dream about had they remained in the United States.

After completion of the Canal, many of the West Indian workers remained on the isthmus and continued to face discrimination, not only by the governing body of the United States in the Canal Zone area but also by the Panamanian government. An example of one of the worst forms of discrimination experienced by these immigrants was in 1941 when, per the Constitution of Panama, they were denied citizenship. Although this was reversed in 1946, the descendants of this segment of society still face discrimination today.

A large number of white citizens in Panama form a very elite group and trace their roots back to the Spanish colonists. They make an effort to maintain the "purity" of their race and keep their inherited wealth by marrying within this tight-knit circle as much as possible. For the most part, they are rich and powerful. Because of their history and economic power, it is no surprise that they became not only the heads of state and successful business owners but also wealthier and more powerful over time. Except during the period of dictatorship in Panama, this elite circle has always been in control of the government.

When the Europeans arrived in Panama, there were more than fifty different Native American tribes. Of the original tribes, only six are accounted for today: the Emberá, Chocó, Kuna, Ngobe-Buglé, Teribe, and Bókatá. The other tribes primarily became extinct because of sickness and their transfer to other parts of the country.

In 2008, the population in the Republic of Panama is estimated at 3,309, 679. Life expectancy at birth is 74.08 years for men and 79.81 for women.[4] The distribution of the population is not uniform, with the majority living in either Panama City or Colón.

Most of the country's population is concentrated in the canal area, cities, and surrounding areas of Panama City and Colón. In the province of Chiriquí, there is also a considerable number of Panamanian citizens, especially along the Pan-American Highway. One-third of the nation's population is located in the urban areas of Panama City, primarily because this is the location of the Panama Canal and the major source of jobs in the country. In recent years, people have left the rural areas and relocated to Panama City in search of work and a better life. The province of Darién is the least populated area, mainly because of the density of the rain forest.

Despite the cultural and ethnic differences that still exist in Panama, there is a strong sense of Panamanian nationalism. The former presence of the United States in the Canal Zone has been one of the major unifying factor in bringing Panamanians of different racial and social classes together.

TRANSPORTATION

Transportation in Panama is quickly changing and improving. Because most of the population cannot afford the expense of a car, the most popular mode of transportation is by bus. Public transportation is efficient in both urban and rural areas, and costs are relatively affordable. In Panama City, for example, the main bus terminal is located in Albrook, part of the former Canal Zone. In addition to local routes in Panama City and it's suburbs, buses are also available to take passengers to the different provinces. Travel to Costa Rica is also possible from this terminal. Many travelers may start their trip in Panama, move on to Costa Rica, and finally reach destinations as far as north as Mexico.

Buses with routes to big cities generally follow a strict schedule, offering a choice of express or local service to urban cities like Colón and Chiriquí. Local buses, on the other hand, do not follow a schedule. They resemble large school buses in the United States, but a difference is the imaginative way in which they are painted and decorated. On each bus, signs show passengers where they are going and music is constantly playing. Occasionally a television may be mounted in a strategic corner in the front for passengers to enjoy the latest releases on videocasette or DVD. To be a passenger on a local bus in Panama City is quite a unique cultural experience.

Taxis are also a very popular means of transportation. Considering Panama's economy, they are an inexpensive luxury. Taxis operate in major cities all over the country. There are no meters, but there is a price control. However, not all drivers follow the rules—some drivers may post prices, others may not, but usually there is room for negotiation.

The Panama Railroad, which dates back to 1855 and for many years was operated by the United States Canal Company, was of great importance to Panama and the world. Its "golden years" were the later years of the California Gold Rush. At that time, the railroad was instrumental in the transportation of passengers from the East to West Coasts. In addition, during the construction of the Panama Canal, the railroad was vital to the excavation process, moving rocks as well as workers from one end of the Canal to the other.

By the end of the twentieth century, the Panama Railroad was no longer the premier mode of transportation between Panama City and Colón. After the Torrijos-Carter treaty was signed, the railroad was returned to Panama but was no longer safe to ride. Under new management, its maintenance declined.

With the change in government and increasing stability in the 1990s, a new railroad line was completed alongside the old in 2001. Its main purpose was to facilitate the transportation of containers between the Atlantic and the Pacific Oceans as well as offer passenger service for the growing tourist industry and for anyone who could afford this luxury, considering the high cost of train travel and the state of Panama's economy.

The second railroad in the country is the Chiriquí Railroad, which operates between the western half of Panama and Costa Rica. It serves mainly the banana industry but also offers passenger service.

With tourism came the construction of more paved roads. The maintenance of these roads has become a priority for Panama's government. Panama's two major highways are the Pan-American Highway and the Trans-Isthmian Highway. Both have benefited from government efforts to improve road conditions in the country. The Pan-American Highway, which starts in Alaska and ends in Argentina, is perhaps the most important on the continent. The Panamanian portion of this highway spans 339 miles. However, the highway between Panama and Colombia ends in Chepo, with an approximately 215-mile gap. The stretch of the Darién Jungle of the Pan-American Highway into Colombia has not been constructed due to the density of the rain forest; in addition, pressure by environmentalists as well as lack of cooperation by the Panamanian government have made this a delicate undertaking. The Trans-Isthmian Highway, which connects Panama City and Colón, is vital to the country because it connects the Panama Canal and the Free Zone, two of Panama's major sources of revenue.

Air transportation has also seen major improvements. *Compañía Panameña de Aviación*, also known as COPA, is one of Panama's major national airlines, offering international passenger service. Panama also has two international airports, both located in Panama City: Tocumen International Airport and the Omar Torrijos International Airport. There are more than one hundred small airports in the country mostly used for transportation inside the country between Panama City and the provinces of Chiriquí and Bocas del Toro, as well as the Free Zone in Colón. With the rise of tourism, major airlines have begun to include Panama as a destination, with several flights per day.

EDUCATION

Education is a central part of Panamanian life, and literacy in Panama, at an estimated 91.9 percent in 2008, has been among the highest in the region. Education is compulsory for all Panamanian youth between the ages of seven and fifteen and is free through the twelfth grade.

The number of years of education in Panama is comparable with the United States', but the structure of the school system in Panama is somewhat different. Panama's system includes an elementary level, *Primaria*, that lasts for six years and is similar to elementary school in the United States. Today, almost all Panamanian children attend the first six years of school. However, there are still problems in the rural areas of the country because of a lack of transportation and money. It can be difficult to get to and from school in these areas, and students sometimes are unable to pursue their educations. Moreover, the degree of poverty is so extreme in the rural areas that children must help work on the farms to contribute and help provide for their families.

Analogous to a United State's middle and high schools are the *Secundaria*, which consists of a middle school level lasting three years termed *Primer Ciclo*, and a second level/high school called *Segundo Ciclo*, which is another three years. The school year runs from April to December, and the public school day varies either from 7:00 A.M. to 12:30 P.M. or from 1:00 P.M. to 6:30 P.M. Some schools have instituted these double shifts in order to accommodate the ever-growing population. Each shift has a totally different set of teachers, students, and clerical and administrative staff.

Most students attend the state-run public school system, although private and religious schools can be found in most large cities. In the public school system, all schools use the same curriculum. At the second level, students have the choice of either an academic or a vocational/technical focus. Academic concentrations differ depending on the student's goals for the university level of education. Once in high school on a specific educational track, students must remain in their track or risk having to start at the beginning. Over the years, high school students have been social activists, organizing protests that have led to violent encounters and tenuous political situations.

In general, students attend elementary and middle schools based on their place of residency; in many cases the cost of transportation is a determining factor, even though students pay a reduced rate to travel to school on the public bus. Because students at the high school level must choose a specialization, they often are forced to go to school in other locations if their choice does not exist close to home or if the school of their choice is overcrowded. To ensure equality in education throughout the republic, with the exception of some private schools, most Panamanian schools are coeducational and uniforms are mandatory.

The number of private schools in the country is increasing. Until recently, most private schools were Catholic, but today a number of primary and secondary nonparochial schools have been established. It should be noted that some schools are linked to churches but not necessarily to Roman Catholic churches, while others have been established by specific ethnic groups.

Schools for the disabled exist in the country, but most are located in Panama City. These include the Helen Keller School for the Blind and the National School for the Deaf. Many parents with children with disabilities have formed groups to assist the government in providing appropriate programs and qualified staff to enhance the education of those with special needs.

In the classroom, the relationship between the teachers and students is very formal, and discipline and mutual respect are expected. Pride in citizenship and public displays of patriotism are encouraged. For example, the *Desfile del 3 de noviembre* (November 3 parade) commemorates Panama's independence from Colombia. During this elaborate celebration, patriotic songs as well as the national anthem are played by marching bands and heard on television stations and radio stations throughout the day. Students who make the *cuadro de honor* (honor role) are decorated with red, white, and blue, the colors of the flag. These students march at the head of the group, representing their schools.

After successfully completing high school, students who have the opportunity to go to university must pass entrance examinations to be accepted in the different areas of concentration, or majors. The acceptance rate depends on availability and number of applicants. As in many parts of the world, numerous university students are activists and are usually at the forefront of political and social change, representing a very important voice for politics and change in the country.

Completion of an undergraduate degree in the humanities or social sciences typically takes four years, and a thesis is required. Professional degrees in law, medicine, or engineering may take between three and one-half to five years. After schooling is completed, the student is granted a *Licenciatura*, the equivalence of a bachelor of science or a bachelor of arts degree.

There are over 350,000 students currently enrolled in various universities throughout Panama. The three oldest and most important university institutions in Panama are the *Universidad de Panamá* (University of Panama), Panama as *La Tecnológica* (Technological University), and the *Universidad Santa María la Antigua* (a private Catholic institution). The University of Panama, which dates back to 1935, has its main campus in Panama City. The Technological University was established in 1975 and was originally the

Engineering Department of the University of Panama. The *Tecnológica* grants bachelor's and master's degrees in the technological and engineering fields. Both the University of Panama and the *Tecnológica* have several satellite campuses in other cities in the country. The *Universidad Santa María la Antigua* was established in Panama City in 1965 and for many years was the only private university in Panama. Panama's progress in the field of education continues with each passing year. A number of small colleges and universities have emerged, including branches of established universities found in the United States. Panamanians are able to make more decisions regarding higher education, and those with money have many choices.[5]

ECONOMY

Panama has a market-based economy that is focused primarily on the service sector. This sector includes the Panama Canal, banking, and the *Zona Libre de Colón* (Colón Free Trade Zone). Together they account for almost two-thirds of Panama's gross domestic product.[6] Commerce and tourism are increasingly playing a significant role in Panama's economy. These factors have made Panama one of the wealthiest nations in Central America and among the most important countries in Latin America.

Since the inauguration of the Panama Canal in 1914, shipping and transport have accounted for the majority of Panama's economic stability. Even when the canal was in the hands of the United States, the Panama Canal Company was responsible for paying the Panamanian government fees for using the waterway. This was a major source of revenue for the country. After the total withdrawal of the United States from the Panama Canal and its passing into Panamanian hands, there was a negative effect on the economy, but in recent years this has diminished. Panama has done a better job than expected in the management of the canal. The United States officially turned the Canal over to Panama in December 1999, and since then, there have been many projects to improve the efficiency of its operation, including the approval of its expansion. This project will shorten the time it takes for a ship to travel the Canal and will allow for the passage of newer and larger ships, a project that is sure to guarantee Panama's importance on the international stage in years to come.

Panama enjoys another source of income by registering many ships; hence it has the largest fleet of ships in the world. There are many benefits of registering a ship in Panama, including lax labor and safety regulations as well as significant discounts on taxes and registration fees. In addition, ships that are registered in Panama pay much lower tolls when going through the canal.

Approximately one-fifth of all vessels that travel in international waters (all are required to be officially registered) are registered in Panama.

The banking sector has also been important to Panama's economy. Workable banking laws and numerous tax exemptions have made it easy for international investors to do business in the isthmus. Panamanians are able to officially use the United States dollar in conjunction with the Balboa, which is the national currency. The Balboa is available only in coins and the United States dollar circulates as the only paper currency. As a result, Panama is an important international financial center.

Located in the province of Colón, the *Zona Libre de Colón* (Colón Free Trade Zone) was created in 1948. It is the second largest free trade zone in the world and a key trading center in the Western Hemisphere, thus playing a vital role in Panama's economy. In the *Zona Libre de Colón*, companies from all over the world are able to import and export goods with reasonable profit, in part because of the reduced tariffs and tax breaks. Its location on the Atlantic coast not far from the port of Cristóbal is an additional benefit.

In recent years, tourism has become a vital part of the Panamanian economy. Panama has the necessary elements to develop a successful tourist industry: warm weather year-round, beaches, rain forests, a free zone, and of course the Canal. Yet because of past corruption in the government, which led to constant instability, and the lack of organization and of any official tourist institutions, this industry was not fully developed. In 1993, the *Instituto Panameño de Turismo* (Institute for Panama Tourism) was formed, and since then tourism has played a major part in the country's economy.

Today the tourism industry is booming, enhancing the country's economy and providing jobs. Tourists come to Panama from other Latin American countries as well as from Asia, Europe, and the United States. The tourism industry is also much more organized, offering custom packages and personalized sightseeing opportunities to suit virtually any interest. Cruise ships from North America not only transit the Canal, as they have done for many years, but now actually make stops in Panama, allowing passengers to disembark and explore the country, further boosting the economy.

Although the land is fertile, a great part of Panama is still virtually untouched. Unlike other countries in the region, agriculture accounts for only 6.6 percent of the gross domestic product.[7] Farming in Panama is limited to a small group of citizens, usually the very poor, who farm basically to feed their families. Panamanians who are involved in farming on a larger scale are mostly concentrated in the western part of the country close to the border with Costa Rica. The area of Cerro Punta is one of the most prosperous regions, producing great quantities of coffee. The region is also important for the banana industry.

Panama's agricultural products include rice, corn, coffee, sugarcane, vegetables, livestock, and shrimp, which are mostly used for national consumption. One of Panama's top export commodities and the major agricultural export for more than a century is the banana. Unfortunately, this industry has not proven to be profitable, as most of its profits have gone to foreign owners for more than a century.

The agricultural sector employs less than 15 percent of the population. Projects such as the trans-Panama pipeline have proved significant to the construction industry.[8] Although Panama is very dependent on world economic stability, its gross national product is among the highest in Latin America. Nevertheless, the wealth that Panama has enjoyed has not been spread equitably among its citizens. Panamanians in the urban areas are much better off than people in the countryside, who are still living in poverty.

As independent and successful as Panama has become from the time the United States handed over the Canal to Panama, its economy is still dependent to a great extent on the United States. A prime example was the devastating effects September 11, 2001 had on the country. Tourism was greatly affected, a domino effect that slowed down trade and tourism and left many citizens without jobs. Yet Panama is still making great progress, and the economy has been progressively improving.

During the last twenty years Panama has been a world exporter of seafood (primarily shrimp), but this has not been stable due to contamination and adverse conditions in the country's fishing industry. Panama also has copper, gold, and silver reserves, but because of strict laws, the mining industry has not been able to operate. In addition, Panama has taken advantage of its many rivers to create hydroelectric plants, which have proven to be beneficial in the production of electricity.

GOVERNMENT

During the first decades of the newly formed republic, Panama's political system was characterized by periods of political instability, premature presidential terminations, and corruption, which led to constant political crises. The modern era of Panamanian politics was ushered in with more than twenty years of military rule that began in the late 1960s and ended with an armed military intervention by the United States. The most recent era of Panamanian politics has seen sixteen years of democratic rule.

From the formation of the Republic of Panama on November 3, 1903, the United States has played an important role in the history and politics of the country. From 1903 until 1986, Panama was basically a constitutional democracy, controlled by an oligarchy. The country saw great changes in the political arena in 1968 when the president, Dr. Arnulfo Arias Madrid, was ousted. A military junta government was in place by the end of 1968, and Brigadier General Omar Torrijos Herrera, commander of the National Guard, became the de facto leader of the country. Even after Torrijos' death in 1981, the country was heavily influenced by the military, and in early 1983 a constitutional amendment was in place to limit the role of the Panamanian Defense Forces (military) in Panama's political life.

Despite the constitutional amendment limiting the role of the military, General Manuel Antonio Noriega became the true force of power in the country by 1983, and the civilian government was left virtually powerless. Panama was in the midst of a political crisis. A long series of events, including an attack on the United States embassy in Panama City and the accusation by the United States that Noriega was involved in the trafficking of drugs, eventually led to the demise of Noriega's regime. However serious these accusations may have been, the event that ultimately led to the overthrow of Noriega's regime by the United States was the annulment of the May 1989 presidential election. The international community, including former U.S. President Jimmy Carter, who participated as an international observer, regarded this election as free and fair.

In order to restore the rule of law and reinstate democracy within the country, on December 20, 1989, the United States invaded Panama (known to Panamanians as *La invación* and known in the United States as "Operation Just Cause"). After the removal of Noriega, Guillermo Endara, the winner of the 1989 presidential election, assumed the presidency and Panama moved to rebuild its constitutional democracy, which continues today and has included the election of Mireya Moscoso, the first female president of the Republic of Panama.

With this tumultuous political cycle behind it, today Panama has three branches of government: the executive, legislative, and judicial. The executive branch is composed of the president, who is chief of state, and two vice presidents elected by direct vote for five-year terms. The legislative branch, also elected by direct vote for five-year terms, is unicameral and has seventy-eight members who are part of the National Assembly. A nine-member Supreme Court, including tribunal and municipal courts, comprises the judicial branch. In 2004 the Constitution was amended, and two major changes will take effect with the national elections of 2009: The executive branch will consist of only one vice president and the National Assembly will not exceed seventy-one members.

HISTORY

The arrival of the Spanish conquistadors and Panama's subsequent inclusion into the Spanish empire in the New World mark the beginning of Panama's modern history. With the passage of time and the realization of the Panama Canal, Panama's history took a markedly different path than those of other countries in Latin America.

Panama: Before Its Independence from Spain

The Spanish arrived for the first time in what is now the Republic of Panama in 1501 during the expedition of Rodrigo de Bastidas, who, in his search for gold, explored the eastern Caribbean coasts of the isthmus.[9] The following year, in his fourth and final voyage to America, Christopher Columbus proclaimed Spanish sovereignty over the region.[10] One of the most prominent figures of the conquest of these zones is Vasco Núñez de Balboa (1474–1517), who crossed the isthmus in 1513, after which it quickly became the crossroads of the Spanish Empire in the New World.

Panama City was founded on August 15, 1519, by Pedro Arias Dávila, who was the Spanish governor of this region of Central America. For years, numerous expeditions for the exploration and conquest of the Pacific-American coast were launched from the port of Panama City. [11] From the sixteenth century until the middle of the eighteenth century, the isthmus region was a strategic route for Spanish traffic on its way to Lima, the capital of the viceroyalty of Peru.[12] As in other Spanish colonies in the New World, colonial life progressed steadily until the nineteenth century.

By the beginning of the nineteenth century, many Spanish colonies in America began their quests for independence from Spain. Panama was not left behind, and on November 28, 1821, Panama declared its independence from Spain and a few weeks later joined *La Gran Colombia*.[13]

Panama, *Gran Colombia*, France, and the United States

President and Liberator Simón Bolivar renounced power on April 27, 1830, as a result of his disappointment about the rivalries and conflicts provoking the separation of the republics forming *Gran Colombia*.[14] His death in December of that year contributed to the political instability of *Gran Colombia*. Coupled with the centralization of economic activities in Bogotá, this was too much for the Panamanian interests in the union, leading to the succession attempts of Panama from *Gran Colombia* in 1830, 1831, and 1840.[15]

The acquisition of California by the United States in 1848 and the discovery of gold in this region the following year were factors that played an important role in the incursion of the United States into Panamanian territory. Both events enforced the need to find a faster and more efficient form of communication between the East and West Coasts of the United States.[16] In the early 1850s, the United States was granted the right to build a transcontinental railroad system across the isthmus; this materialized in the construction of the first transcontinental railroad in the new world. In 1855, the railroad between the cities of Colón and Panama was inaugurated. Although for many years the railroad fulfilled its role of connecting both oceans, it quickly became evident that there was a need for a canal in Central America. For a brief time, the United States considered building a canal in Nicaragua but in the end determined that Panama would be the best site. Many attempts were made by the United States to get permission from Colombia to build a canal in Panama, but none was successful. Instead, Colombia granted the rights to build a canal in Panama to France.

In 1878, the *Compagnie Universelle du Canal Interocéanique* (Universal Company of the Inter-Oceanic Canal), a French company, obtained the rights to build the Canal. On January 10, 1880, under the direction of Ferdinand de Lesseps, the contractor for the Suez Canal in Egypt, the project officially began.[17] Construction of the Canal continued for almost ten years but was suspended at the end of the 1880s and the beginning of the 1890 due to technological setbacks. Outbreaks of epidemics such as malaria and yellow fever had devastating impacts on the workers, hindering construction efforts.[18] Eventually these problems caused a profound economic crisis for the Universal Company of the Inter-Oceanic Canal. The failed company then looked to the United States and favored the idea of the United States negotiating with Colombia for the rights to finish the work on the Canal, but Colombia would not agree.[19]

Panama's Journey toward Independence

The United States remained interested in the construction of the Canal despite the French company's failure. With this goal in mind, the United States proposed the basis for the Herrán-Hay Treaty to Colombia in August 1903. It is important to note that during this time period, the relations between Panama and Colombia had rapidly deteriorated, and Panama was in a state of great unrest because it was seeking independence from Colombia.[20] Although most Panamanians were in agreement that the construction of the Canal should be continued, the Herrán-Hay Treaty was rejected by the Colombian government. When all else failed, the United States intervened in Panama's independence process, with its end goal the signing of a treaty that would permit the United States to build and operate a canal in Panama.

In 1903, the provisional government of the Republic of Panama named a Frenchman, Philippe Bunau-Varilla, as envoy to Washington for the negotiation of a treaty to continue the construction of the Canal by the United States. What the Panamanians did not bear in mind was that Bunau-Varilla was the primary shareholder of the failed French Canal Company; hence he had personal interests in the project that centered on the recovery of monies that he had invested.[21] In the negotiations with the American authorities, Bunau-Varilla took advantage of the opportunity to sign a pact that was favorable to him and came to be known as Hay-Bunau-Varilla. Although, in principle, the provisional government of Panama was opposed to this treaty, it nonetheless gave approval quickly because without approval, it would have risked losing the support of the United States. Were this to happen, it would lose the opportunity for independence from Colombia. In reference to Panamanians and the Hay-Bunau-Varilla Treaty, William D. McCain notes the following: "They were victims of a pact negotiated and signed on November 18, 1903, by an American who knew little of their interest and needs and by a Frenchman who probably cared less."[22]

One of the reasons that Panamanians would later oppose the Hay-Bunau-Varilla Treaty was that, although it permitted Panamanians to become independent from Colombia, it also granted the United States important privileges within the isthmus. For example, the treaty gave the United States the right to construct, operate, and defend the transoceanic canal. Moreover, the Hay-Bunau-Varilla Treaty established the creation of a Canal Zone (a zone about ten miles wide and fifty miles long in the Canal area) under the complete and "perpetual" control of the United States.[23] These concerns became major local and diplomatic issues between the United States and Panama for years to come.

Without another alternative, on November 2, 1903, Panama's provisional government ratified the Hay-Bunau-Varilla Treaty and one day later proclaimed its independence from Colombia. After Panama declared its independence, the president of the United States, Theodore Roosevelt, immediately recognized the new republic and in less than two weeks the United States had the agreement that it wanted. Construction of the Canal began in 1904, and it was officially inaugurated on August 15, 1914.

The United States in Panama

After the United States was granted the right to complete the Canal, the Canal Zone was established. Soon after, military bases were built, and the

Canal Zone housed Panama Canal personnel and their families. These in-cluded mostly white United States citizens, black West Indians, and, in a few cases, Panamanians. The zone had its own schools, supermarkets, post of-fice, and hospitals. It was basically a self-contained area that allowed only the United States to function in the zone. But Panamanian and West Indian work-ers were kept segregated from the United States workers. Life in the Canal Zone was controlled so completely by the United States that an appointed governor was the administrator of the Canal Zone, and U.S. laws were en-forced within the area. All business was conducted in English.

After Panama obtained its independence from Colombia, the United States frequently intervened in the political and economic matters of the new repub-lic. This, coupled with the rights of the United States over the Canal Zone, made the North American presence in the country largely hostile and im-perialistic. This situation provoked various protests and confrontations be-tween Americans and Panamanians. After numerous controversies, on March 2, 1936, the president of Panama, Harmodio Arias, and the president of the United States, Franklin D. Roosevelt, signed the Arias-Roosevelt Treaty, which initiated a stage of revisions to the Hay-Bunau-Varilla Treaty. In 1955, the Eisenhower-Remón Treaty, which was known as a treaty of mutual under-standing and cooperation, was signed. Yet, although both the 1936 and the 1955 documents established important modifications to the 1903 treaty, the Panamanians were not satisfied with the amendments.

January 9 and 10, 1964, saw one of the bloodiest events in Panamanian history and would mark a total change in the relations between Panama and the United States. During the first days of January 1964, Panamanian citizens, among them students, confronted American troops. The main reason for the protest was the failure of the American canal authority to raise the Panamanian flag in public areas of the Canal Zone, as was stipulated in the 1963 Chiari-Kennedy Convention. The confrontation left twenty-two Panamanians dead and more than five hundred injured. As a consequence of this incident, the Panamanian government broke diplomatic relations with the United States, and this ruptured relationship lasted until April 1964.

The events of January 1964 culminated in the revision of the Hay-Bunau-Varilla Treaty and initiated the struggle to have it annulled. After long negotia-tions, on September 7, 1977, General Omar Torrijos Herrera, chief of the Re-publican National Guard of Panama, and the president of the United States, Jimmy Carter, signed a new treaty that was ratified by the United States Senate in 1978. The Torrijos-Carter Treaty recognized Panamanian sovereignty over the Canal Zone and established a gradual transfer of the Canal to Panama that was to be completed by December 31, 1999. Since January 1, 2000, Panama has enjoyed its long-awaited *Soberanía*.

Notes

1. These statistics have been provided by the U.S. Central Intelligence Agency Web site: https://www.cia.gov/library/publications/the-world-factbook/geos/pm. html.

2. Ibid.

3. Ibid.

4. Ibid.

5. Ibid.

6. Ibid.

7. Ibid.

8. Ibid.

9. "Panamá." *Enciclopedia hispánica*. Vol. 11. Barcelona: Encyclopedia Britannica Publishers, 1995: 200.

10. Timothy L. Gale. *Worldmark Encyclopedia of the Nations: Americas*. 9th ed. Vol. 3. Detroit: Gale, 1998: 289.

11. "Panamá." *Enciclopedia hispánica*. Barcelona: Encyclopedia Britannica Publishers, 11, 1995: 201.

12. Timothy L. Gale. *Worldmark Encyclopedia of the Nations: Americas*. 9th ed. 3 Detroit: Gale, 1998: 290.

13. G. A. Mellander. *The United States in Panamanian Politics: The Intriguing Formative Years*. Danville: Interstate Printers and Publishers, 1971: 9.

14. R. Castillero and J. Ernesto. *Historia de Panamá*. 11a ed. Panamá: Distribuidora del Pacífico, 1995: 102.

15. Noris Correa de Sanjur. *Historia de Panamá*. San José, Costa Rica: Litografía e Imprenta LIL, 1995: 117–119.

16. George D. Moffette III. *The Limits of Victory: The Ratification of the Panama Canal Treaties*. Ithaca, New York: Cornell University Press, 1985: 19–20.

17. Elsa María Morales Cordero et al. *Historia 1*. Panamá: Santillana, 1997: 88–89.

18. Walter LaFerber. *The Panama Canal: The Crisis in Historical Perspective*. New York: Oxford University Press, 1978: 13–14.

19. George D. Moffette III. *The Limits of Victory: The Ratification of the Panama Canal Treaties*. Ithaca, New York: Cornell University Press, 1985: 19–20.

20. Gustave Anguizola. *Phillippe Bunau-Varilla: The Man behind the Panama Canal*. Chicago: Nelson-Hall, 1980: 223–230.

21. Jules Dubois. *Danger over Panama*. Coral Gables: Bobbs-Merril, 1964.

22. William David McCain. *The United States and the Republic of Panama*. New York: Russell and Russell, 1965, 33.

23. John M. Lipski. *Latin American Spanish*. London: Longman, 1994, 296.

2

Religion

BECAUSE OF PANAMA'S history as a place of continuous immigration and its geographic location, the country has attracted people worldwide to its shores. These immigrants brought their dreams, customs, and religion with them, creating a cosmopolitan presence and making Panama's religious life unique, with many different faces. Nevertheless, as in most Latin American countries, even today Catholicism is the most popular religion practiced, with an estimated 82 percent of followers declaring it their faith. The other 15 percent are small but significant congregations of other religions that include Baptist, Buddhist, Church of Jesus Christ of Latter-day Saints, Episcopal, Hindu, Jehovah's Witness, Jewish, Methodist, Islam, Bahá'í, and Adventist. These religious groups are represented in the province of Panama, but many can be found throughout the republic. Approximately three percent of Panamanians have no affiliation to any religious group.

Panama's religious panorama has created unusual and interesting clusters of people. As a result, there are Christian and non-Christian groups who are able to meet and practice their chosen religion without fear of persecution, as freedom of worship is allowed in Panama. People of different religious and spiritual views, faiths, religious beliefs, and practices work and live in harmony, thus creating a special element and diversity in the fabric of Panamanian society.

CHRISTIANITY

Ecumenical Committee

There is an Ecumenical Committee in Panama that is made up of three denominations, Roman Catholic, Episcopal, and Methodist, and it is one of the most influential religious organizations in the country. This nongovernmental group plans conferences and interdenominational activities and takes on charitable projects in addition to sponsoring many social, civic, and ethical programs. It works in conjunction with businesses and civic and political groups to address issues concerning Panama. Of particular interest is the Ecumenical Committee's works within this umbrella of institutions that forms the United Nations Development Program—sponsored Vision 2020 in an effort to address issues facing the country and possible solutions to ongoing problems relating to democracy, the economy, ethics, and the environment.

Apostolic Groups

Apostolic churches are also found in the Republic—Apostolism is a Christian Pentecostal denomination. Although they are separate religions, they have similar practices and rituals. They are based in tradition and organization. According to these churches, the bishops and priests continue an uninterrupted succession that dates back to the original apostles. The following churches also subscribe to these beliefs: Roman Catholic, Greek Orthodox, and Episcopal, also known as Anglican. These faiths hold that there are two guides to understanding Christian teaching: the first is the Bible and the second is the knowledge of tradition through the teachings of the priests, saints, and inspired teachers. However, they are all not totally in accord. Both the Episcopal and the Greek Orthodox Churches have issues with succession within the Roman Catholic Church. The Orthodox Church recognized this until the time of separation from the Roman Catholic Church. The Anglicans do not have a problem with this but feel that they must abide by the decision of the Ecumenical Consul.

Panama City is the headquarters of the three Apostolic Churches in the nation. Efforts have been made to unify these churches. However, each has a different leader, and that itself becomes a problem. The pope is the head of the Roman Catholic Church; an ecumenical patriarch and his eleven patriarchs are at the head of the Greek Orthodox Church; and the Episcopal Church has the archbishop of Canterbury and the counsel of the Church in England as its head.

Because globalization is a reality in so many areas of Panamanian life, we also see that the rise and consistent expansion of other faiths is consistently growing. Due to immigration and given the geographic location of the isthmus in relation to the rest of the world, people from the Caribbean, Asia, Europe, and the Middle East have made their way to Panama, and as a consequence, many religious organizations have surfaced over time. Approximately eight percent of the nation belongs to Christian churches that are Protestant, while two percent of Panamanians belong to other organizations. Nevertheless, it is important to consider all of them when looking at religious life in Panama.

Initially, blacks of Caribbean descent made up most of the Protestant church in Panama. This makes sense if we take into account Panama's history and the large immigration from the Caribbean. Because these people came from areas that had been under British rule, they were mostly Protestant. Most of these Protestants were concentrated in Panama City and Colón, the bordering cities on the Pacific and Atlantic entrances of the Canal, respectively.

Roman Catholicism

Strolling, driving, or enjoying a pleasant day in or around the Isthmus of Panama, one cannot help but feel and notice the strong presence of Catholicism. One is aware of the numerous Catholic churches and religious trinkets and the day-to-day religious habits practiced by many throughout the country. This lifestyle is quite popular and readily accepted by everyone as part of the culture, even among those who are not of the Catholic faith.

The vast population of Catholics has its roots in and direct links to the Spanish influence. After the conquest of Panama by the Spaniards, they brought with them not only their culture, foods, practices, and diseases (to which the Indians had no immunity, resulting in the deaths of many) but also Catholicism. From a historical perspective, the rules set forth by the governing body on the isthmus were established by the Spanish monarchs, who decreed that the new subjects, the American Indians, were to be converted to Christianity and as a result would be protected by the Spanish Crown. In theory, this was not what happened. Under many administrators, the American Indians were mistreated and massacred. Some priests were just as violent to the natives as were the Spanish soldiers were, justifying their behavior in the name of God and the conversion of the Indians to Catholicism.

Nevertheless, the American Indians eventually found one priest among the Spanish administrators, Bartolomé de las Casas, who would make a difference. de las Casas made a suggestion to the Spanish monarchy that a change should be made on the isthmus. He said that Africans should be sent in greater numbers to replace American Indians in the Americas, including Panama, basically setting the stage for African slave trade in the New World. After African slaves were transported to the Americas, they were also obligated to practice the Catholic faith and suffered similar injustices at the hands of the colonizers.

Although, in most areas, Catholicism was imposed on the native people of Panama and on the African slaves and their descendants, in Spanish-conquered America, both groups held on to some of their traditional practices. Today, in many areas of the country, several forms of African and indigenous traditional rituals have survived and been passed down from generation to generation. For instance, some Indian groups still use age-old chants and rituals to cure illness and ask for plentiful crops while proclaiming Catholicism as their faith. The reality is that, in recent years, some religions have been forced to become more lenient in matters concerning indigenous traditions to attract more followers. In some areas like the San Blas Islands, missionaries have lived among the Kuna Indians for years, but not all members of the Kuna population have become converts. Moreover, many converts still participate in their traditional religious customs.

Similarly, people of African descent have also found a way to maintain some of their traditions. They have mixed African religious beliefs with Catholicism, creating other forms of religious practices. The fusion of the Catholic faith and African beliefs, especially those from West Africa, developed into different practices among them, two of the most popular of which, *Santería* and *Voodoo*, are still practiced in Panama today. Worthy of mention is the fact that *Santería* and *Voodoo* are also practiced in other countries with histories similar to that of Panama.

Effects of Catholicism on History, Politics, and Culture

The dominance of Catholicism in Panama has been reflected in its history, politics, and cultural traditions. This has been basically the same story for most Latin America countries that at some time were under Spanish rule. Catholicism has left its mark in many areas of Panama's daily life, including politics, history, and culture. There is no clear separation of church and state in Panama's constitution, but it is implied that each functions independently of the other. Yet, it is apparent that for many Panamanians the church forms an integral part of daily life. There was a period when the hold of Roman Catholicism was so dominant that the constitution stated that students in Panama's public schools had to study Catholicism as part of the curriculum. In recent years, this requirement has been minimized, and these courses are no longer mandatory; children of others faiths may be excused.

Over the years, a number of politicians have been quite verbal regarding the church's involvement in politics and have not held back on their criticism of the influence of the clergy on the citizens of Panama. It should be clear that this criticism is not directed toward the Catholic Church as an institution, but rather toward its position from a sociopolitical point of view. One of its most controversial moments was the Catholic Church's involvement in "Operation

Just Cause," when Manuel Antonio Noriega sought refuge and protection from arrest in the safety of the Catholic Church.

Contrary to Panama's policies regarding church involvement in politics, historical documents from the late 1980s describe the role of Archbishop Marcos Gregorio McGrath, a bishop of the Roman Catholic Church, along with other bishops supporting Panama's cry for sovereignty over the former Canal Zone. Under his leadership, there was criticism regarding the Panamanian government's treatment of its citizens and of course the military rule that existed during that time. Archbishop McGrath did not accomplish all that he had planned, yet assistant bishops and other members of the clergy in Panama urged the government to make changes in the manner in which military activities were conducted. On the other hand, over the years, some Catholics have been critical of their local religious authorities.

Popular Catholic Celebrations

The Catholic religion has also influenced daily activities in Panama. Several national holidays are linked to religious celebrations. Among the two most popular are Christmas and Holy Week, which are celebrated on a grand scale in Panama. During these holidays virtually all businesses and government offices have irregular schedules and some are not opened at all to accommodate the employees' holiday celebrations. Another celebrated religious holiday in Panama is All Soul's Day. As in other Hispanic countries, it is a day for recognizing and honoring departed loved ones. Family members usually go to the graves of their deceased family member. At the gravesites, they spend some time in prayer, and flowers and sometimes favorite foods and drinks are also placed on the graves. Visitors and tourists witnessing this tradition for the first time may experience culture shock as cemeteries appear to be transformed into sites of social gatherings.

Catholic religious celebrations such as Easter, Good Friday, and Christmas are celebrated as national holidays. In addition, most communities have a patron saint, and at least once a year there is a local religious procession in honor of that saint. Perhaps the most famous nontraditional Catholic religious celebrations in the republic are the festivals of the *Cristo Negro de Portobelo* (the Black Christ of Portobelo) and *Jesús Nazareno de Atalaya*.

The festival of the *Cristo Negro de Portobelo* takes place in Portobelo every October 21. The are several myths of how the life-sized carved wooden black statue of Christ arrived in Portobelo. One of the most popular is that sometime in the seventeenth century, while the statue was on its way from Spain to Cartagena, Colombia, a storm caused the ship to sink and the statue floated, only to be found later washed ashore on a beach close to Portobelo. Other myths assert that the statue was carved of local wood and was to be shipped to Spain, but unexplainable circumstances prevented this from happening. A third is that the statue mysteriously appeared in Portobelo and each time people tried to move it, they were unable to do so because it became too heavy. Although there is no "official documentation" of its arrival in Portobelo, what is known is that the statue of the *Nazareno* has been on display in the San Felipe church since its dedication in 1814. Legend has it that October 21 was chosen as the day of celebration because sometime in the eighteenth century, a deadly cholera epidemic struck the isthmus and Portobelo residents prayed to the *Nazareno* that the disease did not affect them. In return, the people of Portobelo have a special celebration in his honor on October 21. During the celebration and even the days or months leading up to October 21, many followers who believe in the powers of the *Nazareno* dress in traditional purple robes similar to the one worn by the statue. Several days before the celebration, pilgrims in purple robes can be seen walking great distances on the Tran-Isthmian Highway on their way to Portobelo, some even crawling on their knees as they enter the town. *Nazareno* followers from all over the country and Latin America, and others from as far as the United States and Europe, come to celebrate and take part in the procession. The participants are from all walks and levels of society.

The celebration has three distinct phases. During the first, which starts a few days before October 21, there is a party atmosphere in Portobelo highlighted by gambling and drinking. The second phase starts at eight o'clock sharp in the evening on October 21; at this time, the statue of the *Nazareno* is taken out of the church on the shoulders of eight of its followers and carried through streets of Portobel for approximately four hours. The procession advances as the appointed escorts of the statue slowly make three steps forward and two steps backward; during this time, the *Nazareno*'s loyal followers are able to pin charms on it and admire it as it is paraded through the town. After the statue is returned to the San Felipe church, the party atmosphere is restored and continued until dawn.

Another similar high-profile religious celebration is that dedicated to *Jesús Nazareno de Atalaya*, whose wooden statue is housed in the Atalaya Basilica in a town near Santiago in the province of Veraguas. The celebration is dedicated to *Jesús Nazareno de Atalaya* and takes place on the first Sunday in Lent. The image dates back to the 1730s, when worshippers started visiting Atalaya from nearby areas. Today the annual celebration draws thousands of people from all over the country, many of whom start walking to the basilica on Ash Wednesday. The highlights of this celebration are a procession and a mass at which the high officials of the Catholic Church are in attendance, including Panama's archbishop, the bishop of the Diocese of Santiago, all the bishops of Panama, and the priests of the province of Veraguas.

In July, there is also a celebration in honor of *La Virgen del Carmen,* the patron saint of the island of Taboga. Legend is that pirates tried to attack the island and that while in their ship, they were faced by opposition that was headed by a beautiful woman, the *Virgen del Carmen.* Each July 16 there is a huge celebration on the island of Taboga in her honor. In addition to the traditional processions, the image of *La Virgen del Carmen* is taken out to sea; the boat circles the island in a nautical procession. During these festivities, fishing fleets are blessed and there is a great regatta as part of the celebration.

Today there are Roman Catholic Churches almost everywhere, even in the most remote areas of the republic. Nevertheless, the worldwide problem of the shortage of Catholic priests is also a reality in Panama, which is quite obvious in the remote and rural areas of the country where weeks and sometimes months go by before a priest is able to visit. As a consequence, church attendance in the city areas is much higher than in the rural areas.

In general, Panamanian women tend to be more active in the Catholic Church than men. However, a large number of men are also quite involved in the faith and see to it that their entire family not only attends mass, but also practices Catholicism as an integral part of family life. The other dimension of the Catholic Church is that it serves a social purpose in many ways, as groups of married couples, women, and young people within the church, often interact socially.

Although it is true that today Roman Catholics are the largest religious group on the isthmus and that its members may be found throughout the country at different socioeconomic levels, a number of Panamanian citizens have also found their religious and spiritual ties in a variety of other churches and spiritual organizations.

Other Christian Religious Organizations

It would be difficult to name each individual Christian group in Panama in this book. Many of them are not large congregations and are subgroups of one of the major Christian faiths or have their own special characteristics and beliefs. Because this book is relating the main religions and their impacts on Panama's history, those small groups will not be addressed in this text.

Panama's religious history has the same basic elements as most of Latin America with regard to the Catholic Church. However, based on many unique events over time on the isthmus, including the *Camino Real,* the railroad, and the construction of the Panama Canal, religion in this country has had very different and important moments.

As Panama's history unfolded, many religions continued to grow and make an impact on society on the isthmus. Yet, the long-lasting traditions and influences of Catholicism are ever present, and as per the constitution, Catholicism continues to be the faith of the majority. Moreover, Panama's government respects religious freedom and makes a point to protect this right. To this end, the constitution also makes it clear that all forms of worship are permitted. Nevertheless, the government does not allow its abuse. As a result, overall relations among believers of different faiths are generally good.

Protestantism

The major Protestant denominations present in Panama are the Episcopal, Baptist, and Methodist Churches. During the period of the former Canal Zone, there were a handful of other Protestant denominations, such as Lutherans and Presbyterians, that dissolved after the Canal was turned over to Panama.

The Episcopal Church in Panama is among the largest non-Roman Catholic denominations in the country, with more than 1,500 baptized members in Panama. St. Luke's Cathedral, located in the former Canal Zone, is the Episcopal cathedral. It is made up of over thirty congregations throughout the country. The priests can marry and women can be priests. To date, in Panama, at least three women have held this position.

There are three different branches of the Baptist organization: a church that is affiliated with the Southern Baptist Convention, the National Baptist Church, and the Free Baptist Church. It is not clear exactly how many Panamanians have declared the specific branch with which they are affiliated.

The Methodist Church, on the other hand, is divided into two branches. Although both subscribe to basically the same teachings and beliefs, they function as two distinct churches. One was originally founded by black West Indians who came for the construction of the Canal and today still conduct most of their services in English. The congregation continues to be mostly of West Indian descent. The other is the Evangelical Methodist church, which conducts services exclusively in Spanish. Culturally, this branch is more representative of mainstream Panama.

Like the Catholic religion, many of these other faiths have schools incorporated into their organizations. The Methodist Church, for example, has two well-established private schools: the *Instituto Panamericano* (IPA) in Panama City and the *Escuela Metodista* in the city of Colón.

In recent years, evangelicals have been said to account for more than half of all Protestants in Panama. This is mainly based on the low number of priests in the region and on the fact that the evangelical message is more appealing to people in this part of the world. Evangelicals tend to focus on helping others, and their mission is to share their spiritual beliefs with the rest of the world. This belief fits in well with those of Panamanians. In addition, they have managed to be present in the most remote areas of the country. For instance, they have set up schools in these areas where they teach basic classes along with their religious principles. This is one of the main reasons evangelicals are able to find new converts in the indigenous population and the lower socioeconomic population of Panama.

Jehovah's Witnesses

Other examples of non-Catholic religious organizations that have great visibility on the isthmus include the Jehovah's Witnesses, the Salvation Army, and the Church of Jesus Christ of Latter-day Saints (Mormonism). The Jehovah's Witnesses are known for their door-to-door ministry and the sales of books and *Awake* and *The Watchtower* magazines. This style of spreading the word of Jehovah is practiced worldwide and has attracted many new members. There are more than 139 congregations in Panama, and, as in the Baptist and Methodist Churches in the cities of Panama and Colón, there are usually two groups differentiated by language: an English-speaking group of West Indian descent and a Spanish-speaking group.

Salvation Army

The Salvation Army, an organization that is known worldwide, is also very active in Panama. It provides valuable programs for the disabled, elderly, and poor, among many others. Its mission is based on the revival of Christianity and serving the community.

Church of Jesus Chris of Latter-day Saints

The Church of Jesus Christ of Latter-day Saints, also know as Mormonism, is also one of the fastest-growing groups in Panama, and its presence on the isthmus is directly linked to the Panama Canal. The first Mormons in Panama were linked to the United States military personnel. In the mid-1960s, the Panamanian government officially recognized the Mormon faith in Panama, and conversion in the province of Panama and the San Blas islands began. By the late 1980s, they were well established, but because of deteriorating relationships between the United States and Panama, the American missionaries had to leave. By the early 1990s, new units had been added, and today the Mormons in Panama have eight stakes and six districts (a stake or district is similar to a diocese). In August 2008, the Church of Jesus Christ of Latter-day Saints 127th Temple was dedicated in Panama City, making it the third temple in the Central America area.

NON-CHRISTIAN RELIGIONS

Communities of Muslims, Jews, and Hindus, as well as some Chinese religions, are also found in Panama City and other major cities in the republic. Most of the major faiths have their homes of worship; it is not uncommon to see mosques, synagogues, and temples, but the most famous by far is the breathtaking Bahá'í House of Worship.

Constructed as the Mother Temple of Central America, the Bahá'í House of Worship is one of seven Bahá'í houses of worship in the world. Located in Panama City, it was completed in 1972 and overlooks the Canal. Because the Bahá'í faith's philosophy represents the unity of all faiths, the temple, unlike other places of worship, is open to people of all religions who wish to use it for meditation and prayer. Panamanians take advantage of this. The impressive Hindu temple in Panama City on the Vía Ricardo J. Alfaro is among the largest temples in Latin America.

Of the groups mentioned above, Islam is among the groups with the highest numbers. Muslims have been in Panama from the time of conquest, when slaves were brought to Panama from Africa. Based on their status as slaves, they had virtually no impact. It was not until the period of the construction of the Canal that male immigrants from the Middle East came to work in Panama. It is during this time that there is a marked Muslim presence in the area; of this group, most ended up marrying local women and integrating into mainstream Panama.

At the end of the 1920s, a significant group of Muslims arrived in Panama from Bombay, India. From the late 1920s to the late 1940s, they established an organization called the Sunni Indo-Pakistani Muslim Society and later changed the name to the Panama Muslim Mission. Their most significant work was to start the construction of a mosque in Panama City. There were also other small groups of practicing Muslims in other parts of the province of Panama and in Colón. Between the mid-1960s and early 1970s, the Indo-Pakistani Muslims were teaching their children at home until a program was established in Panama City. It was not until the 1970s that a structured group emerged in Panama City and Colón, and they established prayer and a meeting place in Panama City. On January 15, 1982, the *Centro Cultural Islámico de Colón* was completed, and in 1991 the Muslim community purchased a site that is used as a Muslim cemetery. Today, there are more than four mosques in the country.

The history of Jews in Panama dates back to the colonization era, when Spanish and Portuguese converts were forced to practice their religion secretly. The Kol Shearith Israel, the first Jewish community in Panama, was established in 1876. In 1933, the Shevet Achim Orthodox synagogue and a second Jewish community were established by Sephardic Jews from Israel and Syria. Today, this is the largest Jewish congregation in the country. A second Orthodox synagogue, Beth El, consists of a small congregation of Ashkenazi Jews who came to Panama from Europe in the 1930s.

There are three different Jewish communities and several Jewish organizations that are united under the *Consejo Central Comunitario Hebreo de Panamá* (the Central Jewish Community of Panama). Today, most Jews live in Panama City, Colón, and in David in the province of Chiriqui. Panama now has several kosher establishments, including restaurants and supermarkets, and there are three Jewish schools in Panama City. Panama has had two Jewish presidents, Max Delvalle (1964–1968) and Eric Delvalle Maduro (1987–1988).

The first large number of Hindus came to Panama from the British-ruled Caribbean Islands. Like many others, they came to the country for the construction of the Panama Canal by the United States. Today, Hindus in Panama trace their ancestry to India, Nepal, Pakistan, the Kingdom of Bhutan, and the People's Republic of Bangladesh. The *Sociedad Hindostana de Panamá* is a well-organized, close-knit society with headquarters located close to their Hindu temple in Panama City. In Panama, Hindus are primarily business owners and involved in commercial activities. They are concentrated in the provinces of Panama and Colón, and, in fact, they were instrumental in the development of the *Zona Libre de Colón* (Colón Free Zone).

Like other indigenous communities throughout the Americas, Native Americans in Panama were also forced to accept the Roman Catholic faith to some degree. However, because in Panama the vast majority lived in remote areas and for the most part in isolation, they were able to keep many of their religious beliefs, cultural traditions, and cultural practices intact well into the twentieth century.

In the Native Americans communities in Panama, two of the most significant religions are the Ibeorgun among the Kuna Indians and *Mama Tata* also called *Mama Chí* among the Ngobe, who's population is mainly Guaimí.

In the nineteenth century, missionary activity had begun in some Kuna communities but was not successful. At the beginning of the twentieth century, Roman Catholics and Protestants tried once more to convert the aborigines to the point that by the 1920s, Protestants were officially banned from their efforts to convert them. Eventually these Christian missionaries were able to penetrate the Kuna community, creating two extreme religious groups among the Kunas: those who embraced the new ideas of Christianity and those who refused to be converted.

The Kuna Indians believe in a Papa God and a Nana who is earth mother. The belief is that both Gods first sent all the people to earth and then sent prophets. The most important prophet is considered to be Ibeorgun because he taught them all there was to know about how to live on earth. Their belief is centered around the respect and conservation of nature. They believe that Iborgun lives in the sun and sees everything people are doing. These teachings are transmitted orally through songs and chants. Although today some missionaries and churches have been able to penetrate their society, to a large extent, the Kuna Indians have managed to keep their native beliefs.

As with the Kunas, aggressive missionary work among the Guaymí started at the beginning of the twentieth century. Methodists and Adventists have successfully converted a significant number of natives, but to date the predominant spiritual belief among the Guaymí is a syncretistic religion known as *Mama Chí*. The main belief of the *Mama Chí* followers is that only the Guaymí believers will go to heaven.

The Chocó or Embere Indians have been much more affected by outside influences, specifically by missionaries who use literacy as their religious approach. Most of the converts are born-again Christians.

3

Social Customs and Lifestyle

CUISINE

PANAMA'S CUISINE HAS benefited from the country's tropical weather and surrounding coastline, which create a rich variety of fruits and vegetables as well as seafood and meat, the staple foods of the Panamanian diet.

Some of the fruits and vegetables Panamanians enjoy are avocados, bananas, breadfruit, caimitos, corn, coconut, cumba, guanábanas, mangoes, mamey, mamoncillos, nísperos, otoe, papayas, pineapples, pitaya, plantain, tamarinds, quince, yucca, and watermelon, to name a few. Many of the names of these fruits and vegetables are regional.

As in other Latin American countries, corn is an important part of Panamanian cuisine, on which variety of local foods are based. *Tortillas de maíz* (thick, flat fried corn dough cakes) are usually served for breakfast with cheese melted on top. *Tamal panameño* (made with corn, chicken, pork, and raisins wrapped in leaves and steamed), *empanadas de maíz* (like *tamal*, but deep fried and stuffed with meat), *bollo* (a boiled corn dish), and even *chicha de maíz* (a fermented corn drink) all use corn as their main ingredient.

Although corn is a key ingredient in Panamanian cooking, rice, typically *arroz blanco* (white rice), is served with most meals. It accompanies meat dishes or fruits and vegetables. Some popular dishes are *arroz con coco* (rice with coconut) and *arroz con guandú* (pidgeon peas). As a main entrée, rice is also prepared in a variety of ways. The most popular are *arroz con pollo* (rice and chicken) and *guacho* (rice soup with beans). *Resbaladera* uses rice as its key ingredient, in addition to milk, sugar, cinnamon, and vanilla.

Shrimp, corvina, and lobster are popular seafood items in Panama, as are haddock, red snapper, sea bass, shad, and marlins. At restaurants, seafood is usually prepared *A la Plancha* (barbecued) or *Al ajillo* (in garlic). *Bolitas de pescado* (breaded and fried fish balls), *sancocho de mariscos* (seafood stew), and *ceviche* (raw shellfish and/or fish marinated in lemon juice) are also favorite menu items. Other popular dishes are fish soup and *sopa de mariscos* (seafood soup), made from a variety of seafood.

Beef and chicken are served in a variety of ways. *Sancocho de gallina,* one of Panama's national dishes, is made with cilantro, ñame, onions, oregano, and chicken. Another version, is *sancocho de carne* (meat soup), is made with yams, turnips, carrots, onion, and tropical vegetables like plantain and yucca, in addition to meat. Other popular meat dishes are *guisado,* a stew with meat and tomatoes; *casado,* a beef dish prepared with plantain, rice, and vegetables; and *ropa vieja* (literally translates as "old clothes"), made with pieces of beef and served over rice or yucca. These dishes are prepared in households and restaurants on a regular basis.

There are many small local eateries in Panama. It is not unusual to find one or two people with small shops or food stands selling a variety of low-cost foods. These small shops and food stands are popular for breakfast and lunch. Many of the foods sold are fried, such as yucca, fish, thinly sliced green plantain, *empanadas* (deep-fried dough stuffed with meat, chicken, stew, or cheese), *hojalda,* also known as *hojaldre* (fried dough made of flour), *tortillas* (flat bead from corn or wheat), *carimañolas* (fried cylinder-shaped yucca paste with white ground pork in the center), and *chicharrones* (fried pork rinds). A variety of beverages are available and may include local soda brands like *Malta Vigor* and *Malta del Barú*; *chicha* (tropical fresh fruits mixed with water, sugar and ice); *chicheme* (mashed corn drink to which sugar, milk, honey, cinnamon, and vanilla are added); and *arroz con leche* (rice with milk). *Raspado,* which is similar to a snow cone, is topped with condensed milk and sometimes malted milk, a popular thirst quencher on the frequent warm, tropical days on the isthmus.

Panamanian desserts are outstanding. *Flan* (custard) and *volteado de piña* (pineapple upside-down cake) are part of the cuisine of several Latin American countries, and Panama is no exception. On special occasions, especially weddings, *sopa borracha* (drunken soup) is a must. It is made of pound cake to which cinnamon, cloves, raisins, and rum or brandy have been added. A variation is called *sopa de gloria* (glory soup) to which edible silver bead decorations and whipped cream are added. This is served at *Quinceaños* (similar to a "sweet sixteen" celebration in the United States) as part of the celebration. After a meal, adults often drink coffee.

Other popular desserts are *Plátanos en tentación* (plantains "temptation-style"), made with ripe plantain, butter, sugar, and cinnamon; *manjar blanco* (a caramel-like dessert); and rice with coconut or mangoes or *guandús* (gungo beans).

Panamanians drink a variety of alcoholic beverages and standard mixed drinks such as the margarita, piña colada, and *Cuba Libre* (rum mixed with lime and cola) as well as a variety of beers and rums that are produced locally as well as imported. However, the country's signature drink is *seco,* a Panamanian tequila that is usually poured over ice and milk.

Because of the recent national recognition of Panamanians of African descent, one cannot discuss Panamanian cuisine without mentioning their contributions. In recent years, West Indian cuisine has become accessible to the general public at local restaurants. This very delicious cuisine has always been popular, dating back to the early days of the construction of the Panama Canal. The workers who came from many of the Caribbean islands brought their traditions and culture. They brought some of the fruits and vegetables from their homeland and farmed the ones that could grow in the new soil; consequently, their eating habits continued and were shared on the isthmus.

In the past, West Indian cuisine was not available in established businesses. One would usually find people selling food on street corners, outside their apartments or homes, or while walking in various communities. During special holidays, such as Carnival, the number of vendors would multiply, as it was a time to earn extra money. As the years passed, small bakeries and stores have appeared. Catering is another option for enjoying this cuisine. West Indian food continues to be popular, as it has been for many generations, and there are many upscale restaurants offering a variety of West Indian drinks and dishes. Today, this cuisine has penetrated mainstream Panama, and one of the reasons is the recent passing of the legislation for "Black Heritage" month, celebrated in May. This legislation validates the presence of blacks on the isthmus and the role they have played in making Panama the country it is today.

In restaurants, beverages include *saril* (a red flower that is dried and its petals boiled with ginger, drained, cooled, and sweetened to taste); *icinglass*, made of seaweed with consistency of a milk shake; lemonade; and ginger beer. Entrées include *Escabich* (fish that is fried and marinated in lime juice, vinegar, onions, and peppers overnight); fried fish with rice, *guandú*, and coconut; ackee and cod fish; pigs feet and lima beans with white rice; and *Pepa* (pepper) sauce, a hot and spicy blend of peppers and spices, is always available. Many soups are available, among the most popular of which are cow foot soup, made from the hoof of the cow; oxtail soup; and split pea soup. For dessert, one may order plantain tart, a half-circle-shaped pastry with warm plantain filling; *yucca pone* (grated yucca and coconut milk); and bread pudding.

Because of their isolation, low numbers, and lack of influence on the national stage, Native Americans have had little impact on Panama's cuisine. These natives are mostly hunters, fishers, and gatherers, and, in general, their food is bland and simple; consisting of whatever tropical fruits and vegetables are available in the area at any given time of the year. Fish, banana, beans, corn, plantain, papaya, and yucca comprise a significant part of their diet.

Restaurants are an important element of the Panamanian cuisine experience. In Panama City, there are many types of restaurants ranging from modest and affordable to very expensive and exclusive. Several of the specialized restaurants offer entertainment featuring dancers and musicians.

Panama's history is reflected in its cuisine. Immigrants have cast an international dimension to the country by providing restaurant choices that include Chinese, French, Greek, Indian, Italian, Japanese, and Middle Eastern, as well as other cultural food specialties. American-type food can be found at restaurants like Bennigan's, Burger King, McDonald's, Pizza Hut, Subway, and Wendy's. Many restaurants in Panama that specialize in traditional Panamanian dishes cater to the tourist industry, offering shows with a cultural flair in addition to an exquisite meal.

DRESS

Physical appearance and clothing are important to Panamanians. They take great pride in how they look, especially women. In general, Panamanians have a great sense of style, and both young and old keep up with the current dressing trends similar to what is worn in the United States in warm weather. Blue jeans are very popular and are worn throughout the year. People in the rural areas usually wear simple homemade clothes, sandals, and hats, but this is slowly changing. There is a constant move from rural areas to larger cities in search of work, so many people from the rural areas are adapting to the urban lifestyle and dressing to fit in with mainstream Panamanians.

In the working world, Panamanian women generally wear regular suits or pantsuits, and men wear pants and shirts usually with ties, yet, it is not uncommon to find men wearing *guayaberas* (men's shirts) in pastel colors. *Guayaberas* are made of linen or cotton and have two or four patched pockets. They usually have tucks and embroidery in the front and back, which gives them an elegant look. The retail prices of *guayaberas* are based on the fabric used and the decorative finishes. This allows men of different social and financial levels to purchase the shirts. They are quite fashionable and worn for many social occasions and as work uniforms in some establishments. In some industries (e.g., banks and hotels) and government offices in the public sector, employees are required to wear uniforms.

Pollera

Panama's national dress is the *pollera* (hen cage). The *pollera* is without a doubt one of the most beautiful, elaborate, and expensive national dresses on the South American continent. Like many Latin American national costumes, the *pollera* has its roots in Spain, specifically in Andalucia.

The word *pollera* literally means "hen cage," and there are many stories regarding its origin. The most widespread suggests that the *pollera* was created in Panama and is similar to a type of dress brought to Panama by the Spaniards during the colonial period. Although Spanish women came from different areas of Spain, it is said that the *pollera* is inspired specifically by the clothes worn by Spanish women from the Valencia region.

The *pollera* is a loose, low-cut blouse with an off-the-shoulder neckline worn with a wide skirt with several handmade petticoats. *Polleras* are made of expensive white fabrics such as fine linen, cambric, or voile. They are elaborately decorated with designs of flowers, garland, vines, fruits, or birds. On the more expensive *polleras*, these designs are hand sewn by seamstresses who specialize in *pollera* making. Many work together, and it may take several months to complete one dress. *Polleras* from Los Santos and Herrera, and especially Las Tablas, are considered to be the finest. Depending on the work involved, they are sometimes valued at hundreds—even thousands—of dollars, and the more expensive are handed down from generation to generation.

During the colonial era, the *pollera* was worn by the lower-class women on the isthmus. What exists now is an evolved version of the original *pollera*. Even today, the *pollera* has different categories and varies from region to region. The most expensive and exclusive is the *pollera de gala* (gala pollera) or *pollera de lujo* (luxury pollera), which is worn on special occasions and holidays. It is much more elaborate than the simpler versions, which have fewer, if any, hand-sewn decorations and details. The head decorations that are worn with the *pollera* are also very elaborate. Again, depending on if they are worn with just a regular *pollera* or a *pollera de gala*, the cost and detail can vary. The head decorations consist of several elaborate headpieces called *peines, peinetas,* or *peinetones,* depending on their size. Some are made of gold, pearls, or fish scales. The largest head decoration is usually a comb decorated with pearls and gold, and it is worn toward the back center of the head. *Tembleques*, ornaments made of silver and gold metallic strings, are made to shake on the head. Fish scales and pearls in different designs are also worn. The jewelry worn with the *pollera* can be expensive. Earrings are large and have many different shapes. The jewelry worn on the neck is much more standard. Several long necklaces are worn as a rosary made of pearls or corals, along with a choker with a gold cross on a black velvet ribbon and a gold *cadena chata* (flat chain). Four wide ribbons hang from the waist and pompoms made with wool adorn the center back and front of the blouse. *Babuchas* (satin slippers) are worn with the *pollera*.

Montuno

The *montuno,* which is worn by the men, is said to be of indigenous origin and is less elaborate than the *pollera*. Unlike the *pollera*, which has many different designs and categories depending on location, materials, and handiwork, the *montuno* has only two styles: formal and informal.

The simple *montuno* is a long-sleeved embroidered white shirt with a fringe hanging over simple black trousers. A bag called a *chácara* or *cebadera* and *cutarras* (simple leather sandals) are also worn. The more elaborate *montuno* is a formal, long-sleeved white cotton shirt called a *camisilla* that is worn with black knee-length trousers. The front of the *camisilla* is generally decorated either with rows of tucks or with bright-colored embroidery. Shoes are flat and made of black and white leather. A *sombrero pintado* (painted hat) is worn with both types of *montuno*.

Like the *pollera*, the *sombrero pintado* varies from region to region. The *sombrero pintado*, a straw hat decorated with black designs, is handmade in an elaborate process that sometimes takes several months.

Traditional Panamanian attire is very much a part of contemporary Panama. The *pollera* is often worn during private, local, and national festivities and celebrations. During Carnival season and Independence Day parades, hundreds of Panamanian women wear their *polleras*. Some even wear them instead of traditional white dresses on their wedding days. A celebration called *El desfile de las 1,000 Polleras* (The parade of the 1,000 *polleras*) is organized by the *Instituto Panameño de Turismo* (Panamanian Institute of Tourism) to celebrate the national attire, and it is one of the most beautiful celebrations in the country. In Panama City and Colón, it is not uncommon to see Kuna Indian women in their traditional garments.

In the mid- to late-1980s, tradition and contemporary style came together in a clothing collection, "My name is Panama," that remains very popular today. Kuna Indian *molas*, elaborate panels appliquéd to blouses, shirts, dresses, and footwear, became and remain fashionable.

MAJOR HOLIDAYS AND CELEBRATIONS

In Panama, the New Year is received with an elaborate family dinner called *Cena de Fin de Año* (end-of-year dinner). Young people usually go dancing after dinner. New Year's Day is relatively relaxed, and, because it is a holiday, it is a day for recuperation from the season's festivities and celebrations. In some parts of Panama, it is common to see a figure of a man made of a pair of pants, shirt, and head stuffed with straw, similar to a scarecrow, set on a chair in the front of houses several days before the end of the year. At midnight on December 31, the figure is set on fire, signifying the birth of the new year.

January 6 is *Día de los Reyes Magos* (Day of the Three Kings), and children usually receive gifts on this holiday. In early January 1964, riots broke out between Panamanian students and Zonians (U.S. citizens living in the Canal Zone) who refused to raise Panama's flag at what was then the Canal Zone. On this date, several Panamanians were wounded and more than twenty died. In remembrance of this tragic event, January 9 is designated Martyr's Day.

Carnival

Carnival, a sliding holiday, is celebrated in all of Panama's major cities. The most popular celebrations are in Panama City and Las Tablas. Carnival officially begins four days before Ash Wednesday (anytime between the end of February and March) and ends at dawn on Ash Wednesday, when people go to the beach for a mock ceremony called *El entierro de la sardina* (The Burial of the Sardine).

Although city festivals are becoming very popular, rural festivals are still an important part of Panamanian life. Carnival in Panama is one of the major sources of fun for all ages, and in many ways it is similar to Fat Tuesday in New Orleans. Panama is a fun-loving country, and during the Carnival celebrations, work in Panama literally comes to a stop as the Panamanian citizens enjoy the festivities. Beautiful floats are a major part of the parade. Groups dressed in colorful costumes known as *comparsas* dance in street parades as they beat their drums and play other instruments. Stages and tents line the parade route, and live performers can be found all over the city and communities throughout Panama. They are equipped with powerful loud speakers to keep the festive spirit alive. Street vendors make a great deal of money during Carnival selling food and drinks. Another tradition during the Carnival celebration is the *mojaderas*, also known as *culecos* (getting drenched), when buckets of water, fire hoses, and water balloons are used to wet people in a fun atmosphere.

As mentioned, one of the major cities for Carnival celebrations is Panama City. Official Carnival celebrations in Panama City begin with the selection of the Carnival Queen on the Friday before Ash Wednesday. One of the highlights of the Carnival celebration is the *Pollera* parade on the Sunday before Ash Wednesday. Hundreds of Panamanian women dance, march, and walk around the streets, proudly showing off their *polleras*.

Carnival in Las Tablas is considered by many to be the best in the country because of the elaborate decorations and the detail of the floats and costumes and the quality of the celebrations. Rivalry between *calle arriba* (uptown street) and *calle abajo* (downtown street), with each street tries to outdo the other, makes the occasion even more exciting.

Unlike in the United States, where Easter is the highlight of Holy Week (late March to early April), in Panama, Good Friday processions and reenactments of the death of Christ, especially of Jesus on the cross, are the major events associated with this religious holiday season. Panamanians also observe a number of international holidays that include International Labor Day on May 1 and Columbus Day on October 12. November is referred to as *Noviembre mes de la patria* (November month of the nation) because it has the most national holidays, starting with *Día del Niño* (Children's Day) and National Anthem Day on November 1. November 2 is All Souls' Day. On this day, as discussed in Chapter 2, departed loved ones are remembered by their relatives and friends, who go to the cemeteries and clean and decorate graves with fresh flowers. Some family members may also take the buried person's favorite food or drink to leave at the gravesite.

On *Desfile del 3 de Noviembre* (November 3 parade), discussed in Chapter 1, Panamanians celebrate their official separation from Colombia. The highlight of this day is the elaborate parades throughout the republic. High school students march to patriotic music played by their school bands. They wear *polleras* and *montunos*, the school uniform, or clothes designed for this special occasion usually in red, white, and blue (the colors of the flag). Many government employees also take part in the parade.

Other patriotic days are November 4 (Flag Day), November 10, which commemorates Panama's first call for independence from Spain by an uprising in Villa de los Santos, and November 28, which celebrates Colombia's independence from Spain in 1821, when Panama was a province of Colombia.

Later in the year, on December 8, Panamanian Catholics celebrate the Immaculate Conception of Jesus by the Virgin Mary. As the majority of the population is Catholic, it is not surprising that Panamanians celebrate Mother's Day on the same day. It is not uncommon for mothers to be serenaded in the early morning. Mothers and grandmothers receive gifts and are visited by their children, grandchildren, nieces, nephews, godchildren, and friends. For many Panamanians, Mother's Day is more important than Christmas.

Christmas celebrations take place on December 24 and 25. Homes are decorated with lights, Christmas trees, and extensive *nacimientos* (nativity scenes), to which little figurines are added yearly. As the displays grow, Panamanians take pride in making their mangers the most elaborate. On *Nochebuena* (Christmas Eve), an elaborate dinner is usually prepared, and children are allowed to open their gifts at midnight. Christmas Day is a day of relaxation when children play with their new toys, and grandparents, family, and friends visit.

Additional holidays have been created in the new millennium. Perhaps the most important is *El día de la étnia negra de Panamá* (Black Ethnicity Day of Panama), celebrated on May 30. This celebration pays homage to the black presence in Panama, and the history of the roots of these early inhabitants of Panama are remembered and celebrated.

FAMILY AND GENDER

Both nuclear and extended family members are important to Panamanians. They depend on each other for moral and financial support. The nuclear family usually consists of the father, mother, and children, but it is not uncommon to also have a niece, nephew, or grandparent in the household. The reason for extended families, especially children, living with uncles and aunts is usually financial or educational difficulties. Many families have too many children and cannot afford to take care of them; others live in rural areas where education is poor or nonexistent, so children are sent to the urban areas to go to school or continue their education at the university.

The concept of nursing and retirement homes for the elderly is not a reality for Panamanians. The elder-care industry is in the early stages of development, and family members feel responsible for caring for their parents, and if need be, they even have them come to live with them. Aging parents will generally live at the oldest daughter's home.

If at all possible, most families live in close proximity to each other. Many live in the same apartment building, in the same community, or not far away from each other, allowing for frequent visits. Married Panamanians try to visit their parents often, sometimes daily, and the rest of the family at least once a week. Family gatherings are frequent, even just for Sunday dinner. Celebrations, such as birthdays and major holidays, like Mother's Day and Christmas are usually celebrated within the family.

Children are loved and welcomed in most Panamanian families. But by the time they are seven and eight years old, the social differences and expectations for both sexes become pronounced. For instance, in the rural areas of the country, the rite of passage for a boy usually comes when he receives a *machete* at the age of seven or eight. He is expected to use it, and his priority at that point is to help sustain his family. For this reason, many boys in the rural areas end up not going to school and never receive even an elementary education. Although boys from the poorer sectors in the urban areas do have to work, most start at the end of the school day. City boys usually sell lottery tickets, newspapers, and snacks or shine shoes on the city streets. Unfortunately, in recent years, many of these young boys have become involved in gangs. Boys from the middle and upper class are expected to focus on doing well in school and excelling at sports.

On the other hand, girls from the poorer classes, when not in school, either stay at home to help with younger siblings or work as maids with their mothers. In recent years, many have turned to prostitution as a means of making money. The upper- and middle-class girls are taken care of and generally have no household responsibilities, and like the boys in their socioeconomic class, they are expected to focus on school. Young women are expected to date only one boy at a time and not become sexually active before marriage. Males, on the other hand, generally have more than one girlfriend and are not held to the same standards as girls regarding sex before marriage.

Panamanians in the upper-middle and the elite classes generally celebrate *Los quince años* (a girl's fifteenth birthday). It is one of the biggest *fiestas* the family will ever host. It takes months and sometimes many years to plan this party. It usually begins with a *misa* (mass) at the local church, where the priest prays for blessings for the *quinceañera*, followed by an elegant party where friends and family of all ages come together to celebrate.

The party is preceded by an elaborate ceremony with a court of fourteen of the *quinceañera's* closest female and male friends. These twenty-eight friends perform a choreographed dance, followed by the *quinceañera*, who makes a grand entrance. She has two escorts, usually brothers, cousins, or close family friends near her age and she wears a formal white dress, very similar to a wedding dress but without the train, symbolizing purity. Her escorts wear tuxedos or matching suits, as do the friends in the court. The females generally wear matching long dresses. Also at this ceremony, the *quinceañera* is given high-heeled shoes by her mother and a piece of jewelry by her father, usually a diamond ring. The cake is similar to a wedding cake, with the *quinceañera* and her court depicted on it with little figurines. There is a *brindis* (toast), and the *quinceañera* dances a waltz with her father. After the ceremony, guest are served dinner, followed by dancing all night. The following day, the *quinceañera's* friends visit, and she cuts her birthday cake and opens her gifts, usually personal items, many of which are to be placed in a hope chest in preparation for marriage. The *Quinceaños* celebration varies in cost according to the socioeconomic level of the family. It is easy to spend hundreds, sometimes even thousands, on this celebration. In some upper-class families, the *quinceañera* is given a choice between a trip to Europe or the *Quinceaños* celebration; wealthy *quinceañeras* generally get both.

Both male and female children tend to live at home until they get married. An unmarried girl who becomes pregnant or is a single parent will live at home with her parents and baby indefinitely. If a pregnancy occurs and the couple decides to remain together, married or unmarried, if they are not financially able to take care of themselves, they can live at either of their parents' homes.

For both cultural and social reasons, *bautizos* (baptisms) are important. It is believed that if children are not baptized, the devil or evil witches or goblins can steal the child. For this reason, even people in rural areas go through great lengths to baptize their children, some traveling great distances.

Choosing the right *padrino* (godfather) and *madrina* (godmother) is important because of the opportunities this relationship can provide both to the *ahijado* (godchild) and his or her family. In the lower classes, parents tend to choose *padrinos* (godparents) who are better off than they are, either in terms of wealth or stature in the community. This is done in the hope that they will provide opportunities for the child that they could not have. Godparents may also provide financial support when parents are unable to, paying for schoolbooks, buying clothes, or even putting their godchildren through the university. *Padrinos* (godparents) are expected to be involved in the *ahijado's* religious life and welfare and to play a key role in baptism, confirmation, and marriage. The relationship between the *ahijado* and the *padrino* is formal, and over the years they develop a strong bond. Parents and godparents then become *compadres,* a relationship that carries great significance and family ties. It is a great honor to be asked to be a *padrino*, because this implies respect and trust. It is disrespectful and considered an insult to refuse this honor.

Marital customs vary very much depending on the situation, circumstances, and, in many cases, on social class. In general, marriage is important for the middle and upper classes and less so in the lower economic classes. Also, in the rural areas as well as in the upper-class areas, intermarriage occurs frequently, and in some circles they are actually the norm. Intermarriages ensure that the wealth stays in the family and, in the case of Panama's elite, also preserves racial purity.

Civil and church marriages have never been important to Panamanians in the lower classes. Historically, church and civil marriages have been the norm in the upper, middle, and elite classes. Today, elaborate church weddings are reserved for the wealthy, with more middle-class couples opting to just live together, formalizing their relationship in their twilight years—usually encouraged by their grown children or a priest who convinces the couple that this is necessary for salvation. Children from these unions are not looked on any differently than those from traditional marriages.

There is a rising number of households in which the mother is a single parent and is financially responsible for the family. If she is divorced or separated, she will probably have her mother, a younger sister, or a niece living with her and helping with the day-to-day care of the children. If the woman is young or an only child who never formally left home, she will most likely live with her parents. This situation works for both the aging parents and grown children; as the parents age, there will always be someone left to take care of them.

If, for financial reasons, the woman is not able to go to her parents' house, the paternal grandparents will take in both mother and child. Another scenario is for the mother to leave her children with her parents so that she can work, sometimes moving to major urban areas or even leaving the country to go to the United States. This practice was common in the 1970s and 1980s.

Children who are the products of extramarital affairs, short-term relationships, or divorce do not experience social stigma and are not viewed as illegitimate. Many have close relationships with their stepfathers as well as with their biological fathers, paternal grandparents, and their fathers' other children. In many cases, the father is married and basically lives in two households. Having a *querida* (mistress) is acceptable in many circles. The responsibility the man takes on depends on his class and level of commitment. For example, in the upper and elite classes, the man takes on all expenses and supports both his mistress and children and attends social functions. In the lower classes, although the father will agree to help take care of the child carrying his family name, he will probably do very little (if anything) to financially support his other children.

A woman is expected to have a relationship with only one man at a time, even if he is married and has more than one *querida*. The wife is usually aware of her husband's extramarital affairs, and even if she knows of the existence of other children, she is expected to not question the relationship and to stay with her husband.

In the past, most women in this situation were left with no choice other than to accept these relationships, because, in many cases, they had no financial independence. Under these circumstances, women would take pride in being the *esposa legítima* (legitimate wife), and many developed relationships with their husband's other children, who in many cases were free to visit the house and be a part of family celebrations. Today this is slowly changing, as women are now in the workforce and significantly contributing to household expenses. Women are becoming more outspoken and independent, with little tolerance for infidelity and less willingness to share their funds.

Although the treatment of women in Panama has improved, there are still many hurdles to overcome. At the beginning of the last century, women were not allowed to vote, and very few, if any, were able to attend college. By mid-century, things had improved. Women were given the right to vote, and many were able to attend college. However, discrimination prevailed and continues even today. Although more and more Panamanian women are getting a university education and entering professions that were reserved only for men, gender inequalities still exist. Until recently, women were required to take a pregnancy test before they were hired, and on average, women make half of what men earn for the same job.

With more women getting a university education, they are also marrying and having children later in life. In the rural areas, though, this has not changed significantly. Women in many areas are still expected to get married young or work to support their families, preventing them from going to school and receiving even the most basic education.

In the 1990s, significant changes were made to legislation that benefited Panamanian women. Domestic violence is now a crime, and since the 1997 elections, the law has required that at least 30 percent of all candidates for the legislature be women. In addition, in 1999, Mireya Elisa Moscoso Rodríguez became the first female president in the country during an important time for changes for women.

SOCIAL CUSTOMS

When Panamanians meet each other in social settings, it is expected that the person arriving greets everyone individually, and likewise when the person departs. If Panamanians don't know a person very well, they tend to act very formal. Men shake hands when they meet someone for the first time and give an *abrazo* (hug) to those they have known for quite some time and a kiss on the cheek to women with whom they are well acquainted. Women tend to greet friends and relatives with a kiss on the cheek.

In urban areas, people are polite and cordial to one another. In small towns and rural areas, a nod and a verbal greeting are expected, because most people know or are acquainted with each other. Socializing usually takes place after work, with people meeting at restaurants or cafes. Conversation topics are varied, ranging from sports to the lottery, but almost always including Panama's current political situation.

In the professional world and even at social gatherings, titles are important. It is considered rude not to address university graduates with the proper title of *licenciado* (four-year degree), *ingeniero* (engineer), or *doctor* for anyone with an advanced degree. Even at the primary and secondary levels, students are taught to address their teachers as *maestro* (primary school teacher) and *profesor* (high school teacher). Teachers are respected and regarded as important members of the community, and the titles of *profesor* and *maestro* are retained for life.

After a person passes away, it is common to have a *velorio*, the equivalent of a wake, except that this takes place in the home of the deceased, with the body on display while relatives and friends gather to pray. The *novena* usually takes place the following month, and in some instances the next year.

LEISURE ACTIVITIES

Panamanians are a happy and fun-loving people, as evidenced by the types of activities in which they engage. Panama offers a range of leisure activities that is as diverse as its heritage. Music and dancing are very important. Concerts, festivals, and a variety of celebrations are a part of weekly activities. Nightlife options range from nightclubs to private parties to shows at hotels and restaurants that may include live music and dancing.

Panamanians also enjoy going to the movies. Although Panama City has several venues, this form of entertainment is still very limited in most areas of the country. Most movies shown in theaters in the United States eventually make it to Panama, sometimes several weeks after they have been off the screen in the United States. Panamanian law requires that all foreign language films be subtitled in Spanish.

One of the most popular activities in Panama is playing the *lotería*. The *Lotería Nacional de Beneficencia* (National Lottery for the Benefit of Panama) was created in 1883. It requires that 64 percent of all ticket sales be paid to winners; prizes range from one dollar to several thousands. Lottery tickets are sold all over the country at all times, usually by people employed by the government on the sidewalks of busy public places. It is not uncommon to be in a restaurant, a beauty salon, or even in a hospital lobby and be approached by someone selling *billetes* (tickets). Panamanians of all social sectors engage in this nationally promoted gambling activity, and some buy tickets every week of the year. Because Panamanians are very superstitious, some buy specific numbers that represent something significant in their lives; it could be a birth date, house number, or a number related to a dream they had. The drawings are transmitted live on major local channels and radio stations on Wednesdays and Sundays. When the drawings take place, the country becomes almost paralyzed, with everyone tuned in for the results.

Citizens and visitors enjoy gambling in casinos, which are found all over the country, especially in Panama City. New casinos have been opening at an astounding rate. In the past, major hotels had casinos as part of their establishment, along with nightclubs and restaurants. Today, casinos are a major part of the hotel business, occupying a lot of physical space and providing a major source of profit. In recent years, several casinos have become to stand alone as individual businesses.

Cockfights and horse racing are also popular in Panama. Cockfights take place all over the country, but the Province of Chiriquí has the greatest number of gamecocks and cockfight arenas. The major fights are on holidays and on Saturdays and Sundays. Horse races are held on Thursdays, Saturdays, Sundays, and holidays at the José A. Ramón Race Track in Panama.

SPORTS

Because of Panama's tropical weather, its citizens enjoy and participate in a wide variety of sports year round both as active participants and spectators. As in many parts of the world, sports are still a male-dominated activity. Baseball is by far the most popular team sport in Panama. This is partly because it is a simple sport that requires only a stick and a ball. Panamanian children are introduced to baseball early in life, and it is not uncommon to find children playing in parks or even during school lunch breaks. Soccer is also gaining momentum as a group sport, as evidenced by the recent appearance of soccer clubs and organized tournaments all over the republic. Panamanians follow the World Series closely. Young men participate in junior league competitions, and Panama even has a National Junior League that competes at regional and international Junior League World Series Tournaments.

Gambling associated with sports, cockfights, and horse and greyhound racing is popular in Panama. In the early 1970s, professional boxing gained prominence in Panama when *Manos de Piedra* (Hands of Stone) Roberto Durán managed to put his country on the map. This was a positive distraction; Panamanians were struggling with politics associated with the Panama Canal at this time and needed something to celebrate. Many Panamanian world champions followed, making this sport one of the most popular in the country as well as a source of great pride for the Panamanian people.

As Panama becomes more of a vacation and retirement destination, sports that were practiced but were not necessarily widespread (mostly because of cost) and specialty sports are appearing. Water-related activities and water sports have expanded: diving, fishing, scuba diving, snorkeling, surfing, swimming, and white water rafting are just a few. Cycling, tennis, hiking, and horseback riding are also growing in popularity. Golf especially has become increasingly popular, with a handful of golf courses in operation, and more are being built.

SIGNIFICANT FIGURES

Since the second half of the twentieth century, Panamanians have made a name for themselves both on the national and international stages, especially in politics and history, as well as in entertainment and sports. In recent years, three of the most outstanding Panamanian figures in the national and international political and historical arenas have been Omar Torrijos Herrera, Mireya Elisa Moscoso Rodríguez, and Manuel Antonio Noriega. From the late 1960s to 1981, Colonel Omar Torrijos Herrera controlled Panama. After only eleven days in office, in 1968, Torrijos was able to force newly elected

Panamanian president Arnulfo Arias Madrid out of office. Brigadier General Omar Torrijos Herrera formed a council and made himself Panama's ruler, remaining the dominant force behind Panamanian government until his unexpected death in 1981. Torrijos was a controversial figure who, on the one hand, was a harsh dictator but, on the other hand, did a lot to improve education, housing, and health in Panama, benefiting mostly the poor and rural population who where among his major supporters. He also helped to put Panama on the international business arena when he opened banking to foreign companies tax-free and exempt of related fees. These benefits are still present today.

Torrijos became a national hero when he convinced the United States to agree to turn over the Canal and the Canal Zone to Panama. In 1977, U.S. president Jimmy Carter and Omar Torrijos Herrera signed canal treaties that would gradually give Panama control of the Canal Zone starting in 1979 and total control of the Canal and Canal Zone by 1999, an historical event for Panamanians who had long awaited their *Soberanía total* (total sovereignty). During his time in power, he was able to turn the Panamanian Defense Forces into the most powerful political body in Panama.

After Omar Torrijos Herrera's death in an airplane crash in 1981, an elected civilian government was put in his place. Nevertheless, by 1983, Manuel Antonio Noriega was the head of the Panamanian Defense Force. He quickly became the strongman in Panama and was controlling the government. Initially, Noriega worked with the Central Intelligence Agency (CIA) as an informant in matters concerning Colombian drug dealers. By the mid-1980s, this relationship started to deteriorate, and by February 1988 Noriega was indicted by the United States for drug trafficking. After several years of corruption and criticism of the United States, in early December 1989 Noriega declared himself head of the government and declared that Panama was at war with the United States. Panama made the international news headlines later in December that year when "Operation Just Cause" was put in motion. On December 20, 1989, U.S. president George H. W. Bush deployed 27,000 United States soldiers to Panama to capture and arrest Noriega for money laundering and drug trafficking. The mission was accomplished and Noriega was convicted.

After serving more than fifteen years in prison in the United States, Noriega was to be released in September 2007; but in August of that year, a United States federal district court judge approved his extradition to France. In France, he was convicted in absentia for money laundering and was also convicted in absentia in Panama for murder and Human Rights violations. Today, Noriega remains in prison under United States custody awaiting results from an appeals process over French extradition.

After the lessons learned with Torrijos and Noriega, Panamanians eliminated military forces in the country. They have been replaced with the Panamanian Public Forces, divided into four independent groups: the Institutional Protection Service, National Air Service, National Maritime Service, and Panamanian National Police. All four organizations were headed by civilians.

From 1999 to 2004, Mireya Elisa Moscoso Rodríguez was president of Panama. She was the first female president of Panama and the second in the region. She is also a symbolic figure because she was Arnulfo Arias' widow (Omar Torrijos had forced Arnulfo Arias out of office in 1968) and won the presidential election against Martín Torrijos, Omar Torrijo Herrera's son. Ironically, Mireya Moscoso was also the Panamanian government's official representative in the ceremonies of the turnover of the Canal in 1999, which was previously signed by Omar Torrijos Herrera.

In the political arena, the most recent figure is President Martín Torrijos Espino, son of former Panamanian dictator Omar Torrijos Herrera. Like his father, he received support from the rural population and the poor during his campaign. To date, his most important project has been the laying of the foundation for the expansion of the Panama Canal, a project that is well on its way receiving the go-ahead from the Panamanians following a national vote. Presidential elections are scheduled for May 3, 2009 and the elected president is to take power in September 2009 until 2014.

In the areas of music and entertainment, Rubén Blades is one of Panama's best-known performers. He is a multitalented individual who has been an outstanding actor, composer, singer, and songwriter. He has received several Grammy Awards and has recorded over twenty albums. Blades has appeared in several movies and has been instrumental in the dissemination of salsa music in Latin America and in the United States. His hit *Pedro Navaja* is the best-selling salsa single of all times. He is also a political and social activist: after earning a law degree, he later received a master's degree in international law from Harvard Law School. In 1994, he came in third in Panama's presidential election, and, in 1999, he was appointed to be one of seven Goodwill Ambassadors to the World Conference Against Racism by the United Nations. In September 2004, he was appointed minister of tourism by Panamanian president Martín Torrijos.

Another outstanding singer and musician is "El General" (Edgardo A. Franco), who was instrumental in popularizing Spanish reggae, and he is also considered by many to be the father of what today is known as *Reggaetón*. El General was awarded Billboard's first-ever award for "Best Latin Rap Artist." The Panamanian musical group Los Rabanes was nominated for a Latin Grammy for best rock interpretation. Another outstanding artist is Danilo

Pérez, whose production *Mother Land* was nominated for the Grammy Latino 2001 in the category of "Best Jazz Interpretation"; although he did not receive the award, *Mother Land* was named best record of the year by the *New York Times* and also received the Boston Music Award.

Lesser-known Panamanians who have been distinguished with awards include Omar Alfano, who was named Composer of the Year at the Billboard Latin Music Awards in 2001; and José Quintero, who won two Tony Awards: the first in 1957 for his production of *Long Day's Journey into Night*, the second in 1973 for best director for *A Moon for the Misbegotten*.

In the last three decades, Panamanian folk music has been revitalized and has become part of modern music trends in the country. Panama's folk musicians have also stepped out of Panama to make their mark on the international stages. Osvaldo Emilio Ayala, also known as *El Escorpión de Paritilla* (the Scorpion of Paritilla), is Panama's best-known accordionist and has taken his music all over the world. In more recent years, Samy and Sandra Sandoval, a brother-and-sister team also known as *Los Patrones de la Cumbia* (the masters of cumbia), have been the ambassadors of Cumbia inside and outside Panama.

Sports in Panama are an important form of recreation, and its most successful players have been a great source of pride. Panamanians have been outstanding in many sports but have been most successful in baseball and boxing. Baseball has produced excellent Panamanian players who have made it to the major leagues in the United States. One of the most famous is Rodney Cline Carew (Rod Carew). In 1967, when Rod Carew began his professional career with the Minnesota Twins, he was selected as the American League Rookie of the year. He also won seven batting titles and was selected Most Valuable Player in the American League in 1977. In 1991, Rod Carew was inducted into the Baseball Hall of Fame, and Panama's National Stadium is named in his honor.

Other outstanding Panamanian sports figures in baseball are Juan Berenguer, Bruce Chen, Manny Sanguillen, and Mariano Rivera. In 1999, Mariano Rivera was voted the Most Valuable Player in the World Series while playing for the New York Yankees.

Boxing has also had its fair share of Panamanian champions. Many boxers have won world titles and some have even made it into the Boxing Hall of Fame; they include Teófilo Alfonso Brown, "Panamá Al Brown" (1992), Eusebio Pedroza (1999), and Ismael Laguna, *El tigre de Santa Isabel* (2001) and Roberto Duran.

Considered by many to be the best lightweight boxer of all times, Roberto Duran *Manos de Piedra* (Hands of Stone) is without a doubt among Panama's greatest athletes. In Duran's forty-year boxing career, he was lightweight, welterweight, light middleweight, junior middleweight, and middleweight world champion. He fought his first professional fight at the age of sixteen and his last professional fight when he was fifty. At that time he had 104 wins, 69 knockouts, and 16 losses.

Other international Panamanian sports heroes include Laffit Pincay Jr., who participated in and won the Kentucky Derby in 1984, and runner Lloyd La Beach, who received two bronze medals in 1948.

The year 2008 was especially important to Panama as Irving Saladino became the first Panamanian to win a gold medal at the Olympics. Saladino also know as *El Canguro* (the kangaroo), won the gold medal in the men's long jump Olympic Games of Beijing, China by jumping 8.34 meters (27 feet, 4.5 inches). Panamanian president Martín Torrijos has publicly promise that the future *Ciudad del deporte* (sport city) will be named in his honor.

4

Literature

THE RELATIONSHIP BETWEEN Panamanian literature, history, politics, and popular culture is important. Panama's literature developed in close relationship to its history, which "officially" started with the arrival of Europeans to the isthmus. During the colonial period, its literature was tied to the actions of the Europeans, who had become the dominant group on the isthmus. After separating from Spain in 1821, Panama became part of Colombia, and later the United States would have a permanent presence on the isthmus. It is not surprising that when Panamanians started writing, their work reflected a burning desire for sovereignty. The literature that emerged kept a watchful eye on the realities of everyday life, the adverse effects of the foreign presence in Panama, the influence of the United States, and national patriotism.

EARLY WRITERS

Literature about Panama began with the discovery of the isthmus, and although natives did not write this literature, it is significant because it provides valuable information about Panama before and during the period of colonization. Precolonial literature appeared in the form of letters and reports of Europeans who were exploring Panama for the first time. In his *Carta de relación del cuarto viaje* (1503), Christopher Columbus wrote about his fourth voyage to the New World and mentioned the area that would later become Panama. According to his *Carta de relación del cuarto viaje*, Columbus and his crew explored Panama's coast from November 1502 until May 1503.

Vasco Nuñez de Balboa (1475–1519) is credited with the discovery of the Pacific Ocean and was present for the founding of Santa María la Antigua. He also wrote objectively about Panama in his *Carta de referencia* (1515), comparing its physical beauty with that of other locations in the Indies.

Other Spaniards who wrote about Panama, focusing on the day-to-day events during the colonial era, were Gaspar de Espinosa (1465–1537), Martín Fernández de Enciso (1469–1537), and Pascual de Andagoya (1498–1548). Espinosa led many brief attacks on Panama and was known to be the first European to walk on isthmian soil. He also founded Natá and wrote about its population. In 1510, Enciso founded Santa Maria la Antigua del Darien and traveled extensively on the isthmus. *Suma de geografía*, which he wrote in 1518, offers the first insights to Panama's botanical and animal life. Andagoya was a Spanish conquistador who worked with Pedrarias, Balboa, and Espinosa. He spent several years in the region and was among the first to write about Peru's greatness. His *Relación de los sucesos de Pedrarias en la tierra firme y de los descubrimientos en el Mar del Sur* is valuable because of the great detail it provides about these historical events.

As Spain began to establish itself in Panama, literature started to take the form of historical accounts, a contrast with early literature from the isthmus, which focused mainly on personal narratives of the newly discovered land. These accounts presented a more accurate and organized version of what was happening in the New World. The importance of different events became quite evident, as did the need for accurate documentation. During this period, Pedro Mártir de Anglería, Fernando Colón, Fray Bartolomé de las Casas, and Pedro Gutiérrez de Santa Clara all made valuable literary contributions about Panama.

Pedro Mártir de Anglería (1475–1526) is recognized as the author of the first history of America based on the letters, accounts, and writings of others who had visited the New World. His *Décadas del nuevo mundo* is especially important because it provides detailed accounts of some of the most important moments in Panama's early history. Fernando Colón (1488–1539), Christopher Columbus's son, accompanied his father on his fourth voyage to the New World. He wrote about this experience in *Vida del Almirante*, which included testimonies from his father and others who were with him on this voyage. Fray Bartolomé de las Casas (1474–1566), a Spanish priest and the first bishop of Chiapas, is known for his opposition against the enslavement of the natives in the New World. An historian and a scholar, he provided valuable details about Panama during this period in *Historia de las Indias*, one of his most important works. The most important document written at the time, however, was Gonzalo Fernández de Oviedo's *La Historia natural y general de las Indias,* which contained the most information on Panama during the colonial period.

As Spain continued with its exploration, discoveries, and colonization in the Americas, Panama's importance increased. Because of its strategic location, Panama, even in this early stage, was already considered a crossroads of the Americas. Although Spain had imposed strict literary censorship in the New World during the colonization period, in practice it was difficult to enforce this in Panama because of the volume of people and goods that crossed the isthmus on a regular basis.

There is some documentation from 1545 indicating that Panama received books from Spain. Even during this time, some references to Panama were appearing in Spanish literature. One of the most important was written by the famous Spanish writer Lope de Vega, whose epic poem "La Dragontea" deals with Sir Francis Drake's last expedition and attack on Nombre de Dios. Panama is also mentioned in his famous work *La Dama Boba.*

During the period leading up to the appearance of the first works actually written by Panamanians, there were several Spaniards who lived or traveled throughout Panama. They gave detailed accounts of life in Panama and its people as well as general descriptions of different aspects of the isthmus as they saw or experienced them. These writers include Don Bernardo de Vargas Machuga (1555–1621), Juan de Miramontes y Zuázola, Pablo Crespillo de Ovalle (1595–?), Lucas Fernández Piedrahita (1624–1688), and Fernando de Ribera (1591–1646). Other writers were much more detailed in their documentation, providing valuable and concise information. In *Sumaria descripción del reino de tierra firme* (1575) and later in *Descripción de Panamá y su Provincia* (1607), Alonso Criado de Castilla (?–1611) provided information on Panama's population as well as its physical and geographic properties. In addition, he covered topics related to Panama's name, economy, politics, and history.

Antonio Vásquez Espinosa's (15??–1630) most important work is *Compendio y descripción de las Indias Occidentales* (1628). It contains important documentation about Panama's history, economy, and social life. Juan Requejo Salcedo (?–1646) had been involved in work for the Catholic Church in Panama and was commissioned to write *Relación histórica y geográfica de la provincia de Panamá* (1640) about the ecclesiastic life in Panama. Likewise, Diego Ruiz de Campos was commissioned to write *Relación de la costa panameña en el Mar del Sur* (1631), which focuses on aspects of Panama's geography. Francisco Silvestre (1734–?) wrote *Descripción del Reino de Santa Fé de Bogotá,* concentrating on such topics as the population, history, and politics of Colombia, Ecuador, Panama, and Venezuela.

THE NINETEENTH CENTURY

Literature written by Panamanians did not appear until the end of the nineteenth century. By this time, many Panamanians were not only able to travel to Spain but were also able to attend the university there. Later, when educational institutions were established in Panama, more citizens were able to get formal educations. At that time, the most important academic institution in Panama was the San Javier University, established by the Jesuits.

With formal education, Panamanians were able to actively participate in the writing of literature. Víctor de la Guardia y Ayala's "La Política del Mundo" (1772–1824) is the first known literary work of value by a Panamanian. It is a tragedy in verse in three acts that criticizes Napoleon for invading Spain. It appeared in Penonomé in 1809. Another noteworthy Panamanian during that time was José de Antequera y Castro, who successfully translated several classic Latin works into Spanish.

Other important Panamanian writers during this period were Manuel Joseph de Ayala (1728–1805), considered by many to be the most outstanding jurist of his time because of the extensive coverage and in-depth topics and aspects of law he presented in his works about the colonial times. Dr. Sebástian López Ruiz (1741–1832), a medical doctor and naturalist, is considered to be among the most outstanding in his field because of his scientific monographs. His work in the sciences, especially in the discovery of new plant specimens, was an invaluable contribution.

After obtaining its independence from Spain, Panama was part of Colombia from 1821 to 1903, a time of many changes on the isthmus. With the construction of the railroad and the initial attempt of the construction of a canal, Panama provided many work opportunities to people from all over the world. Because of its status as a center of transit, it did not take long for Panamanians to become protective of their country, developing a strong sense of patriotism that translated into a need for autonomy and ultimately independence from Colombia. As a result, at the end of the nineteeth and the beginning of the twentieth centuries, a strong sense of Panamanian nationality emerged, which was displayed in many ways—among them in literature.

When Panama first became part of Colombia, and with the introduction of the printing press and circulation of local newspapers, many people wrote poems and published them. Most wrote about political situations and in many cases challenged Panama's position as part of Colombia. Nevertheless, the most significant writings on the isthmus at the time were by Mariano Arosemena (1794–1868) and later by his son Justo Arosemena (1817–1896). Both men wrote a series of essays on key moments in Panama's history.

Mariano Arosemena was considered by many to be a neoclassical writer, but his importance in Panama is based on his work as a journalist and an historian. He founded *La miscelánea del Istmo* (1820), the first newspaper in Panama, and he used it to promote his ideas about Panama's independence from Spain. Mariano Arosemena also played a key role in politics. On November 28, 1821, when Panama received its independence from Spain, he was among the Panamanians who signed the proclamation of independence act. He was senator for the *Gran Colombia* in 1825 and served as plenipotentiary minister in Peru in 1852. He is further known for his historical studies. His *Apuntes históricos*, covering Panama's history for the first twenty years of the nineteenth century, is the only one of its kind and is considered priceless. Mariano Arosemena is considered by many as the first Panamanian historian.

Like his father, Justo Arosemena was heavily involved in politics. He was a lawyer by trade, and his contribution to Panama's literary tradition lies in his essays. Although he wrote many essays, "Comentario al Proyecto de Acto Reformatorio de la Constitución" (1852) and "El Estado Federal de Panamá" ("The Federal State of Panama") (1855) are considered his most important works because of their content and the sociohistorical perspective they offer. They reflect on Panamanian history and nationality and provide arguments in favor of the creation of a federal state, all of which are significant and provide the basis for further studies on the subjects.

What followed was the first significant group of poets on the isthmus, known as the *Primera generación poética*. They were considered by many to be the first literary generation in Panama. The *Primera generación* wrote during a time when Romanticism was at its peak in Europe and was starting to appear in literature in Latin America. The ideas of revolution, nationalism, and independence expressed through Romanticism were embraced and developed by authors of Romanticism in the New World, as were politics and history. This fit in perfectly in the New World, because in the 1900s, the height of Romanticism, many Spanish colonies were receiving their independence.

Romanticism

By 1821, Panama had received its independence from Spain and become part of Colombia. Many events took place during that time, including the building of the railroad and later the Canal by the French and then the Americans. Based on Panama's political and historical situation at that time as part of Colombia, the strong presence of the French, and later the Americans, it was only natural that as Panamanian literature developed, a theme expressed by writers was the need for reform.

Romanticism, the major literary movement at the time, developed differently in the various countries in Latin America. Because of Panama's unique political situations during this period, poetry in this region dealt with political and historical issues. Among the writers we find are Gil Colunje, Tomás Martín Feuillet, and Amelia Denis de Icaza.

Gil Colunje's (1831–1899) ode "28 de Noviembre" about Panama's independence from Spain focuses on nationality and is said to be the first poem of literary value written by a Panamanian. His novel *La verdad triunfante* is considered to have initiated the development of the novel in Panama. In addition to writing, he was also involved in politics, holding several important public offices. He was a journalist and the founder of several newspapers, including *El centinela* (1856), *La tribuna federal* (1879), and *La defensa* (1880).

Tomás Martín Feuillet's (1834–1862) is said to be one of the best representatives of Romanticism in Panamanian literature. He wrote several poems that captured the spirit of the Romantics: depressing, sad and pessimistic, all of which characterize his poetry. His poem "Flor del Espíritu Santo," dedicated to Panama's national flower, articulates his deepest sentiments and is considered to be one of his best pieces.

Amelia Denis de Icaza (1836–1911) is Panama's first official female poet. Her poetry focused on political and social issues. She spent most of her life outside of Panama, traveling and living extensively in Central America. In 1906, toward the end of her life, she visited Panama and was appalled at the situation in the country. She was especially disappointed with the role of the United States and its presence in Panama. Icaza was upset that the United States had control of the territory known as the Canal Zone and was displeased by the disadvantageous situation of Panama as it related to the Canal. As a result of these situations, she was moved to the point that she wrote the poem "Al Cerro Ancón." This was her way to protest and express regret and pessimism about the future of Panama. She has become one of the country's most symbolic poets.

Also of importance for this first generation of writers is José María Alemán (1830–1887), whose theatrical play *Amor y suicidio* (1876), about an impossible love with a sad ending, is considered the second-best-known play in Panama's history. In addition, Alemán's *Recuerdo de juventud* (1872) is thought of as the beginning of literary criticism in Panama; this piece included twenty poems and literary studies on several Panamanian authors.

Before Panama's independence from Colombia, poet and journalist Manuel T. Gamboa (1840–1882) published *El céfiro* in 1866. *El céfiro* became Panama's first newspaper dedicated exclusively to the fine arts—the first *periódico literario*—and Gamboa the first literary critic of value. *El céfiro* was also key for the Panamanian poets of the Romantic period, as they were able to have their poetry recognized.

Transitional Writers

The *Primera generación poética* (First Poetic Generation) was followed by a group of poets who, like the group of writers before them, also dealt with aspects of Panama's national realities. The main difference between Panama's first generation of poets and those who followed was that, in general, they were much more interested in the social values of poetry and tended to focus even more on aspects of Panama's contemporary political and social realities. In literary terms, they are called "transitional writers," because we find aspects of both Romanticism and modernism in their writings, as their work has important social and national components. These writers include Jerónimo Ossa, Federico Escobar, and Rodolfo Caicedo.

Jerónimo Ossa (1847–1907), a civil engineer, wrote Panama's national anthem. Ossa wrote several poems in many different weekly publications and magazines during his lifetime. Although his poems were simple, they were nationalistic and focused on Panama.

Federico Escobar (1861–1912), Panama's first black poet, was also known as *El bardo negro*. He went through both movements. Although he received very little education, he rivaled many writers of his time. Federico Escobar started out with Romantic tendencies and evolved to become one of Panama's greatest modernist poets. As he developed, he eventually accepted the changes of the times, and his poems became some of Panama's best examples of modernist poetry. He was especially proud of his black race, which was reflected in his writing. In addition, in keeping with his times, he wrote about social and political issues, as well as poems on popular culture and Panamanian life.

Rodolfo Caicedo (1868–1905), another transitional writer, wrote about the glories of the Panamanian nation. Although he did write poetry, he is best known for his fables, which he used to criticize politics and society.

Unlike poetry, which rapidly flourished in Panama, prose was slower to develop. As we mentioned before, Gil Colunje's novel *La virtud triunfante* (1849) is considered the foundation of the novel in Panama because it was the first serious attempt at the novel genre in Panama. *La virtud triunfante* is a typical romantic novel about a wealthy young lady (Julieta) who falls in love with a young man (Cesarino) who does not belong to the same social class.

After *La virtud triunfante*, many short stories and novels started to appear in newspapers, although they were not of the highest quality. Among the novels that did receive attention was Soledad Acosta de Samper's novel *La perla del valle,* which was published in *El céfiro* newspaper in 1866, R. Álvarez Gori's *Un sueño*, which was published in the *El crepúsculo* literary newspaper in 1870, and Jeremías Jaén's *Mélida*, which was published in 1888. In 1889, Manuel José Pérez published *El último delirio de Byron,* and, in 1895,

Edmundo Botello and Abel Ramos published *Novela exótica*. It was not until Julio Ardila's (1865–1918) *Josefina* (published in 1903) was written that the Panamanian novel was "formally" established.

TWENTIETH CENTURY

Modernism

Modernism took off in Latin America at the end of the nineteenth century and the beginning of the twentieth century. This movement consisted of a new attitude toward life, a rejection of the past, and, in a way, the embracing of a new identity. The Nicaraguan writer Rubén Dario, who is considered to be the head of modernist literature in the New World, visited Panama several times and helped promote the movement on the isthmus. By the time modernism found its way to Panama, writers were inspired by all things national.

By the time Panama had successfully negotiated its independence from Colombia and signed a treaty to have the United States continue the construction of the Canal, the modernist movement had replaced Romanticism in Panama. Overtones of modernism started to appear in the different forms of Panamanian literature.

Among the most important writers of this modernist period were Darío Herrera (1870–1914), who became the best-known Panamanian writer outside of Panama. Herrera had the opportunity to travel extensively in South America, including to Buenos Aires, which was the meeting place for modernists in America. He moved in the same circle as Leopoldo Lugones and James Freyre. Herrera wrote poetry and short stories but was most famous for his short stories. In 1903, *Hojas lejanas* was published, making it the first short story book written by a Panamanian.

Other important writers during this period were León A. Soto (1874–1902), known mostly because of his mastery of the sonnet; Demetrio Fábrega (1881–1932), whose poetry is deemed outstanding; and Salomon Ponce Aguilera (1868–1945), whose short stories are considered the first stories of any significant literary value in Panama. Also, Guillermo Andreve (1879–1940) established a series of publications in which authors could publish their work; these included *Cosmos*, *La revista filatélica*, *El Heraldo del Istmo*, and *La Prensa*. Andreve's most important contribution to literature in Panama was the establishment of *La biblioteca de la cultura nacional* (1918), a collection of thirty-six booklets in which the most important literary pieces of the time were published.

After Panama's independence from Colombia, poetry continued to flourish in the new republic. Its most important figure during the first five years of independence was Ricardo Miró Denis (1883–1940), considered to be Panama's greatest poet. His publications include *Preludios* (1908), *Los segundos preludios* (1916), *La leyenda del Pacífico* (1924), *Versos patrióticos y recitaciones escolares* (1925), *Caminos silenciosos* (1929), *El poema de la reencarnación* (1929), and *Antología poética* (1937). His best-known poem, "Patria," was written in 1909 while he was in Spain and is memorized and recited by students in school all over the country. It is a tribute to Panama, "Patria" focuses on the nostalgia of his motherland, but because of the manner in which it is written, the poem transcends Panama to encompass any nation. Ricardo Miró's importance is such that the literary prizes in the country for most outstanding essays, novels, poetry, and short stories are named in his honor.

One of the most outstanding and purest writers of Panama's modernist period as well as the youngest was Gaspar Octavio Hernández (1893–1918). He was the only black author of this period. He started to work at a very young age, and consequently he did not receive a formal education. Despite the challenges he faced, including the color of his skin and his lack of a formal education, he managed to gain employment as a journalist and later as the editor in chief at a local newspaper, *La estrella de Panamá*, one of Panama's most prestigious newspapers at the time. His poems are filled with modernist characteristics, focused primarily on themes of social injustice, nationalism, and popular culture of the time. As did Federico Escobar, he often made reference to the realities of being black in a society that was dominated by whites. He wrote two books of poetry, *Melodías del pasado* (1915) and *La copa de Amatista* (1923), and he also wrote valuable essays, short stories, and many literary critiques on the writings of several authors.

After the period of modernist Panamanian literature, a group of new authors emerged who were called "transitional" because their writing could be categorized in any one movement (modernist or vanguard).

Not to be overlooked is María Olimpia de Obaldía (1891–1985), also known as "La Alondra Chiricana," whose work has been difficult to categorize. She has come to be considered the feminist representative of the postmodernist era in Panama. She was the first woman allowed to be a member of the *Academia panameña de la lengua*, and, in 1930, a national tribute was held in her honor, at which she was proclaimed "María Olimpia of Panamá." Her poems focused on themes associated with women (children, motherhood), emotions, and everyday life. Her books of poems include *Orquídeas* (1926), *Parnaso infantil* (1948), and V*isiones eternas* (1961).

Considered a modernist writer by some and a transitional writer (between modernism and vanguard) by others, Demetrio Korsi (1899–1957) was the most important poet of his generation. Although he wrote poetry for most of his life, his best work was written toward the end of his life. He wrote about popular aspects of everyday life in the capital city, with a special focus on Santa Ana (a popular neighborhood in Panama City). Among his most renowned poems about Panama are "Block," "Cumbia," "José el tamborero," "Los poemas extraños," "Pequeña antología," and "Visión de Panamá."

Other poets of this "transitional" period were Ana Isabel Illueca and Santiago Anguizola Delgado. Ana Isabel Illueca (1903) wrote about patriotic and regional aspects of Panama, specifically on the *campesina* (country woman); poems such as "Flor simbólica" (which makes reference to Panama's national flower, *La flor del espíritu santo*), "Mi pollera," and "El Montuno" (Panama's national dress) are among her most popular poems. She also wrote children's poems.

Santiago Anguizola Delgado (1898–1980) was from the province of Chiriquí, and his poetry is almost exclusively about that province's natural geographic landscape and regional characteristics. His two major poems are "Rayos de luna" (1933) and "Soy chiricano" (1956).

As literature developed and was refined on the isthmus, there were obvious and positive changes in Panama's literature. The creation of the annual Ricardo Miró Literary Prize in 1942 marks an important aspect of Panama's literary development. This contest was originally created to recognize the work of writers, and later not only to improve the quality of writing but also to encourage the production of literature in Panama. At its inception it consisted of three first, second, and third prizes for three categories and had a modest monetary sum attached to the prizes. Over the years, the award has gone though several modifications to what it is today: one prize for each of five categories: poetry, short story, novel, theater, and essay, each with a monetary compensation of U.S. $15,000 (significant for Panama) and a gold medal. To date, this is the most prestigious literary contest in the country.

Vanguard

By the 1920s, vanguard started to appear on the European literary stage, and it remained strong for another twenty years. The vanguard, also known as the avant-garde movement, flourished during a crucial time in the world, between World Wars I and II, and in Latin America, in addition to literature it was also reflected in painting and plastic arts. Like the literary movements before it, vanguard made its way to Panama at a similar time in its history, because, in the 1920s and 1930s, Panama was undergoing several economic and social national crises. As a literary movement, the vanguard's main goal was the renovation of literature and liberty in writing and the breaking away from the traditional forms or conventions by creating absolute liberty for the artist.

Rogelio Sinán's (1902–1994) first book of poems, *Onda* (wave), marked a turning point in Panamanian literature. Sinán, who had lived outside of

Panama since 1924, had been exposed to the latest literary trends in Europe, and while he was in Rome in 1929, he published *Onda*. In this work, he incorporated an unusual and different way of expression that introduced and served as the initiator of the vanguard movement in Panama. After his return to Panama, Sinán gave presentations on literature and aesthetics, which enhanced this movement and served as a foundation for the new direction literature was taking in the country. Like the title anticipates, *Onda* created a wave in Panama's literature. Although his work in *Onda* was revolutionary, he is best known for his book of short stories, *La boina roja y cinco cuentos* (1953), which has long been considered among the best short story collections in Mexico and Central America.

Demetrio Herrera Sevillano (1902–1950) also embraced the vanguard movement; two of his most famous poems that have also become Panamanian classics are "Cuartos" and "Tú siempre dices que sí." In "Cuartos," Herrera Sevillano describes the pitiful conditions of the rented rooms where people were forced to live in Panama, while "Tú siempre dices que sí" is a poem in which he criticizes Panamanians for always saying "Yes" and accepting injustice. Along with Demetrio Herrera Sevillano, other popular Panamanian poets who continued the development of the vanguard movement are Ricardo J. Bermúdez Alemán (1914–2000), Stella Sierra, Eduardo Ritter Aislán (1916–2006), Tobías Díaz Blaitry (1919–2005), Matilde Real (1926–?), Elsie Alvarado de Ricord (1928–2005), José Guillermo Ross Zanet (1930–?), and Bertalicia Peralta (1939–?). Most of these writers and their work have been recognized at some point either by their winning the Ricardo Miró Literary prize in the category of poetry or their winning international literary poetry contests.

Short Stories

By the 1930s, literature had picked up in Panama, and a series of high-quality short stories and novels started to appear. The themes, characters, and plots were often related to the typical Panamanians of the time. Most of the best authors had been recognized for their novels or short stories but not for poetry, not necessarily because this genre was nonexistent before the vanguard movement, but rather because they were not that good. The short story was form that was the most developed during this period and, authors were generally placed in one of two categories: *Regionalistas* (regional) or *Urbanos* (urban).

Regionalistas *and* Urbanos

Writers who fell into the *Regionalista* category wrote stories about a specific region of the country, parts of the country that many Panamanians knew little or nothing about. The writers were usually from the region about which

they wrote, or they were familiar with the traditions, legends, and social realities of that area because of their experiences within the culture of the specific region. The second group of short story writers developed works which
focused on Panama's "urban" life; that is to say, the major metropolitan areas. Panamanians who have been successful at writing short stories that fit
in these categories include Rogelio Sinán, Ignacio J. Valdés, Lucas Bárcenas,
José María Sánchez, Carlos Francisco Chang Marín, César A. Candanedo,
Roque Javier Laurenza, Roque Javier Laurenza, Álvaro Menéndez Franco,
Pedro Rivera, and Ernesto Endara.

Rogelio Sinán, who wrote under the pseudonym Bernardo Dominguez
Alba (mentioned earlier), is also considered one of the greatest Panamanian
writers of the twentieth century. His first book of short stories, *A la orilla de
las estatuas maduras* (1932), set the course for the novel genre in Panama, and
the story "La Boina Roja" from his book *La boina roja y cinco cuentos* (1953) is
considered his best short story. In 1944, Rogelio Sinán published his famous
poem "Incendio," which was inspired by a fire in his neighborhood, and one
year later, in 1945, he published his book of poems *Semana santa en la niebla,*
for which he was awarded the first prize in the Annual Ricardo Miró Literary
contest. In 1969, he published a collection of his poems, titled *Saloma sin
salomar.* In addition, he received awards for his novel *Plenilunio* and wrote
plays for children, including *Cucarachita Mandinga* (1937) and *Chiquilinga*
(1961).

Another famous short story writer was Ignacio J. Valdés (1902–1959). He
was originally from the province of Veraguas, and his *Sangre criolla* (1943)
and *Cuentos panameños de la ciudad y el campo* (1957) both include short
stories that focus on the reality of Panamanians who live in rural sectors of
the country. One of the main themes was the people who would leave to go
to the "city," which would ultimately cause a disintegration of the provincial
system. From Arraiján in Chorrera, Lucas Bárcenas (1906–1992) also wrote
short stories about characters from the rural sector of the country who were
frustrated because they had no hope of fulfilling their dreams of having the
basic necessities of life. He wrote "La flor," "Las diez velas del Santo," "La
camisa del señor alcalde," "La puerta cerrada," and "Un chombo."

José María Sánchez's (1918–1973) most representative short stories of
Panama are set in his native Bocas del Toro. He won the first place prize
of *La Estrella de Panamá,* a local newspaper's Christmas Story, in 1947 for
"Embrujo de navidad," and in 1948 for "Una aclaración necesaria." Carlos
Francisco Chang Marín (1922–?) is from the province of Veraguas and has
won the Ricardo Miró contest several times in the categories of short story,
poetry, and novel, as well as several international literary competitions. He has
also written children's literature and popular *décimas*, which is a poetry form

that is octosyllabic and has ten lines. His most important short story collection is *Fragual y otros cuentos* (1978); in recent years he has published other books of short stories, including *Nochebuena mala* (1995), about the invasion of Panama by the United States in 1989; *Las mentiras encantadas* (1997); and *Cuentos para matar el estrés* (2002). Originally from the province of Chiriquí, César A. Candanedo (1906–1986), who wrote under the pseudonym Gil Serrano, worked as a sanitary inspector, which gave him the opportunity to travel extensively through Panama. He was successful at integrating his knowledge of different regions of the country into his writings. For instance, in *Los clandestinos* (1959), he wrote about people who entered Panama illegally via the bordering province of Darién.

Roque Javier Laurenza (1910–1984) is most famous for "Los poetas de la generación republicana" (1933), a lecture at the National Institute during which he spoke against the poets of the republican period. His literary work is considered valuable because of its innovative style. His most popular short story, "Muerte y trasfiguración de Emiliano García," was published in Ricardo Miró's *Antología del cuento en Panamá* (1950). In 1969, Pedro Rivera (1939–?) became the first writer to win first place in both the short story and the poetry categories of the Ricardo Miró literary competition for "Peccata Minuta" (short story) and "Los pájaros regresan de la niebla" (poetry). In recent years, he has co-written *El libro de la invasión* on the Panama invasion of 1989 and won the Ricardo Miró literary competition for poetry in 2000.

Ernesto Endara (1932–?) has won the Ricardo Miró competition on several occasions. Most recently, in 2001, he won the Rogelio Sinán Central American Literary contest for his book of short stories *Receta para ser bonita y otros cuentos*. Álvaro Menéndez Franco (1939–?) has also won several national and international competitions for his short stories.

Novels

Unlike poetry and short stories, the novel genre struggled to find its place in Panama even after independence from Colombia. It was not until the 1920s, mainly as a result of literary contests, that novels of any literary value started to appear. After production picked up, the novels in Panama are now divided into several categories based on theme.

The first is composed of the novels categorized historically based on the subject they discuss. Octavio Mendez Pereira's (1887–1945) *El Tesoro del dabaibe* (1934), reprinted as *Vasco Núñez de Balboa* (1934), is a biography of Vasco Núñez de Balboa, and *Tierra Firme* (1942), about Panama during colonial times, are included in this category. Julio Belisario Sosa's (1910–1946) novels *Tú sola en mi vida* (1943) and *La india dormida* (1948) both received prestigious literary prizes. *Tú sola en mi vida* is about life in Panama at the beginning of the 1930s. *La india dormida* is about the resistance of Urracá and other Guaymí Indians to Gaspar de Espinosa in the Veraguas mountains. One of the most popular novels that fits this category is Gil Blas Tejeira's (1901–1975) *Pueblos perdidos* (1962), a historical novel about Panama from 1882 to 1914.

At the same time, a second group of novels emerged. Their focus was on social and political realities of Panamanian life, usually occurring in the city. Joaquín Beleño's (1922–1988) *Luna verde* (1950) is about injustices Panamanian workers endured; Narciso Navas's *Panamá, novela político-social* (1924); Renato Ozores's *Playa honda* (1950); and Mario Riera's *Rumbo a coiba* (1947) all deal with aspects of contemporary Panamanian life.

It is also easy to identify a third category that focused on national heroes, like José A. Cajar Escala's (1915–1994) novel *El cabecilla*. Others, like Rogelio Sinán's *Plenilunio* (1947) and Tristan Solarte's *El ahogado* (1957), go into a more psychological realm. Ramón H. Jurado's (1922–1978) novels *San Cristóbal* (1943), *En la cima se mueren los Suicidas* (1950), *Desertores* (1951), and *El desván* present Panamanian social issues to some degree.

A group of more contemporary writers who wrote in the vanguard style and are worthy of mention belong to a more recent generation that has woven sociopolitical issues into their writings, dealing primarily with the Canal Zone and the United States' invasion of Panama in December, 1989. Among the best known of these writers are José de Jesús Martínez (1929–1991), also known as Chuchú. One of his last works was *La invasión de Panamá*, which provided a detailed description of this invasion. José Franco (1936–?) has written well-received novels on the Canal Zone situation, *El panteón de los callejones* and *Good Bye USA*. His most famous poem is "Panama defendida." Diana Morán (1932–1987) wrote *Soberana presencia de la patria* (1964). Maravia Ochoa (1939–?) wrote *Juan Garzón se va a la Guerra* (1992), another book of stories related to the invasion of Panama by the United States in December 1989.

In recent years, most of Panama's best writers have won the Ricardo Miró literary contest or some other prestigious international literary contest at some point. Like several writers in Latin America, most Panamanian writers have professional degrees (doctors, lawyers, architects) and are usually well educated and well traveled, and their writings tend to focus on contemporary sociopolitical issues primarily written in narrative form. Among these contemporary Panamanian writers who focus primarily on the narrative form are Javier Alvarado, Justo Arroyo, Ariel Barría, José Manuel Bayard Lerma, Giovanna Benedetti, Rosa María Britton, Errol E. Caballero, Sydia Candanedo de Zúñiga, Eustorgio Chong Ruiz, Enrique Chuez, Ernesto Endara, Carlos Fong, Ramón Fonseca Mora, Gloria Guardia (1940–?), Mireya Hernández,

Enrique Jaramillo Levy (1944–?), Dimas Lidio Pitti, Griselda López, Gilma Noriega de Jurado, Maravia Ochoa López, Antonio Paredes Villegas, Allen Patiño, Bertalicia Peralta, Rafael Pernett y Morales, Pedro Luis Prados, Pedro Rivera, José Luis Rodríguez Pittí, Rafael Ruiloba Caparroso, Isis Tejeira Jaén, Consuelo Tomás, Beatriz Valdés Escoffery, Carlos Oriel Wynter Melo, and Boris A. Zachrison.

Most contemporary poetry in Panama has been published in local magazines and newspapers and has also been included in several national and international anthologies. In this group are Pedro Correa Vásquez (1955–1995), Héctor Miguel Collado (1960–?), Giovanna Benedetti (1949–?), Consuelo Tomás (1957–?), Vivianne Nathan (1953–?), Luis Pulido (1961–?), Porfirio Salazar (1970–?), José Carr (1958–?), Sonia Ritter de Fledderjohn (1940–?), and Ramón Fonseca Mora (1952–?).

Two Panamanian writers have been considered for nomination for the Nobel Prize in Literature. Moisés Castillo Ocaña (1899–1874) was owner of the famous literary newspaper *Miscelánea* and creator of the Ricardo Miró literary contest. Álvaro Menéndez Franco (1933–?) also won numerous prizes. Franco's most-read work is his poem "Panamá Defendida," which is about Panama, but from a patriotic perspective; it also focuses on the negative circumstances associated with the presence of the United States in Panama as well as on the exploitation of the native Indians.

Afro-Panamanian Writers and Writings

Panamanian writers of African descent have made valuable literary contributions to Panama. From as early as the beginning of the twentieth century, Panama has recognized their efforts and hard work. The first prominent black writer in Panamanian literature was Federico Escobar (1861–1912), also known as *el bardo negro* because of the dark color of his skin, and *el carpintero poeta,* because he worked as a carpenter during the construction of the canal by the French. As mentioned earlier, his poetry usually falls in the transitional period between romanticism and modernism. Pride for his race and his profession are recurring themes in his poetry. He wrote *Oda a Cuba* (1902), *Hojas secas* (1890), *Instantáneas* (1907), and *Patrioticas* (1909). He also wrote two stage plays, *La lLey marcial* and *La hija natural.*

No study of modernism in Panama would be complete without including Gaspar Octavio Hernández's (1893–1918) poetry. His mastery of versification made him a key figure in the development of modernism on the isthmus. Self-taught and the youngest writer of the modernist period in Panama, he was also the editor-in-chief of *La estrella de Panamá* newspaper. He died at the age of 25. Like Federico Escobar, Gaspar Octavio Hernández's poetry included issues of being black in a predominantly white-controlled society; he also wrote on injustices committed mainly by the United States in Panama and dedicated some of his poetry to popular culture. Among his most famous poems we find "Azul," "Cantares de Castilla de Oro," "Canto a la bandera," "Cristo y la mujer de Sichar," and "Ego sum"; these poems appear in his two books of poems, *Melodías del pasado* (1915) and *La copa de amistad* (1923), published after his death.

Two writers who were successful at presenting issues of racial conflict for people of African descent in Panama are Rogelio Sinán (1902–1994) and Joaquín Beleño (1922–1988). In his two novels, *La Isla Mágica* and *Plenilunio*, and his short story "La Boina Roja," Sinán was able to integrate aspects of racial problems in Panama. Joaquín Beleño's trilogy *Luna verde* (1941), *Curundú* (1963), and *Gamboa Road Gang* (1960) also focus on issues relating to race in the Panama Canal, especially of the English-speaking West Indian blacks and their descendants in the Panama Canal Zone.

In more recent years, there have been many different forms of literary expression from Panamanians of West Indian descent, most exploring aspects of the Afro-Panamanians as individuals and as a community, including facts from both the past and the present. Earl V. Newland and Joseph Dixon have been successful at writing poetry in English, and Alberto Smith Fernández and Carlos E. Russell have produced valuable poems in the Spanish language. Others have been successful at bilingual productions; among them we can find Melvin Brown's (1956–?) book of poetry *Legado/Heritage* (1988) and Melva Lowe de Goodin's play *De Barbados a Panamá/From Barbados to Panama* (1999), both focusing on the lives of West Indians in Panama.

Another outstanding contemporary Panamanian writer of African descent is Gerardo Maloney (1945–?). Gerardo Maloney is a sociologist who has been the director of *Radio y televisión educativa*; he has written several poems and published essays on Panamanians of African heritage. His work includes a book of poetry titled *Juega vivo* (1984).

Writing under the pseudonym of Cubena, Carlos Guillermo Wilson is perhaps the most important contemporary Panamanian writer of West Indian descent. Novelist, poet, and scholar, he has published three novels, *Chombo* (1981), *Los Nietos de Felicidad Dolores* (1991), and *La misión secreta* (2004); *Cuentos del negro Cubena* (1977), a collection of twelve short stories; and *Pensamiento del negro Cubena*: *Pensamiento afro-Panameño* (1977), a collection of poems. His most recent publication is *Raíces Africanas, Los mosquitos de Orixá Changó cuentos y novelas* (2005). Cubena has successfully re-created historical, political, and social realities of West Indians and their descendants during and after the construction of the Panama Canal. But his subject matter is not limited to those events—he has incorporated the shared history and the struggle of people of African descent throughout the world.

Other Afro-Panamanians who have been successful at literary writing include Armando Fortune (1921–1979), Diógenes Cedeño Cenci (1927–?), Juan Moterno Vásquez (1927–?), Ricardo Segura (1938–2002), and Winston Churchchill James (1956–?).

NOTE

Much of this section on literature is based on information found in two sources, *La literatura panameña* (San José, Costa Rica: Imprenta Trejos Hermanos, 1972), written by Rodrigo Miró, and *Panorama de las literaturas hispanoamericana y panameña* (Panamá, República de Panamá: Ministerio de Educación, 1983), written by Emilia R. de Ramirez, Gladys B. de Ayala and Susan R. de Torrijos.

Panama City skyline. © Mortenelm/Dreamstime.com.

A large ship moves through the canal. Courtesy of the author.

View of Panama City skyline. Courtesy of the author.

So-called mules are dragging a ship through the narrow Gatun Locks of the Panama Canal. © Ramunas/Dreamstime.com.

A container ship is escorted by tugboats through the Culebra Cut next to the Centennial Bridge in the Panama Canal. © AP Photo/Arnulfo Franco.

Exterior of San Felipe Church in Portobelo, where the *Cristo Negro* (Black Christ) is housed. Courtesy of the author.

Cristo Negro de Portobelo statue inside San Felipe Church. Courtesy of the author.

Palacio de las Garzas (Herons' Palace), where Panamanian presidents reside. Courtesy of the author.

Cathedral reconstruction in Old Panama. © Rjlerich/Dreamstime.com.

A view of San Jose Church or Altar de Oro (Golden Altar), on Casco Viejo in Panama City, Panama. © AP Photo/Arnulfo Franco.

Young boy wearing a *guayabera* and *montuno* hat. Courtesy of the author.

Young girl in Panamanian folkloric attire. Courtesy of the author.

Woman wearing the *pollera de gala*. Courtesy of the author.

Panamanian family of West Indian descent enjoys a Sunday meal at home. Courtesy of the author.

A traditional Panamanian breakfast: beef, *tortilla de maiz con queso blanco* (corn tortilla with farmer's cheese), *hojalda* (fried dough), and *café con leche* (coffee with milk). Courtesy of the author.

A Diablo Sucio character dances through the streets during the Corpus Christi nine-day celebration, in Villa de Los Santos. © AP Photo/Tomas Munita.

Panamanian elementary students attend the 2007 opening class ceremony in Canita. © AP Photo/Arnulfo Franco.

Revelers dance under a spray of water during Carnival celebrations in Panama City. © AP Photo/Tomas Munita.

Traditional Kuna Indian house. © Rjlerich/Dreamstime.com.

Fort of Portobelo. © Koubatian/Dreamstime.com.

Fish *mola*. © Traveler1116/Dreamstime.com.

A Ngobe-Bugle woman carries her baby during a rally in Soloy. © AP Photo/Arnulfo Franco.

A semi truck travels alongside a new locomotive of the Panama Canal Railway in Corozal. © AP Photo/Jaime E. Yau.

Public bus drivers protest throughout the main streets in Panama City, Panama. © AP Photo/Arnulfo Franco.

Kuna Indian women watch the movement outside of a voting station during general elections in Panama City. © AP Photo/Dario Lopez-Mills.

5

Media and Cinema

MEDIA

THE REPUBLIC OF Panama has a broad range of print and electronic media outlets that include newspaper, radio, and television and, in more recent years, cable and Internet. The development of media in Panama has been different than in other Latin American countries because of the uniqueness of its location: it has been a magnet for people from all over the world for centuries. Most important to the media development in Panama has been the "official" physical presence of the United States in the country in the form of military bases in the Canal Zone.

Perhaps one of the most challenging and significant moments for the media in Panama was the period from the early 1970s to the early 1990s, when basically all forms of media coverage in the country were controlled or regulated by the military regimes of Omar Torrijos, Rubén Darío Paredes del Río, or Manuel Antonio Noriega. During those military periods, the United States' media coverage of events was especially significant for Panamanians because it offered a different perspective on what was going on in the country.

The end of the twentieth century and the beginning of the twenty-first brought many positive changes to this industry by offering greater variety and providing more services to Panamanians, further promoting globalization in the country. Nevertheless, there is not as much freedom of the press as was projected, and to a great extent high government officials still have the power to have journalists put in jail for criticizing them.

Newspapers

With the help of Simón Bolivar at the beginning of the nineteenth century, many Spanish colonies were being emancipated, and it was precisely Panama's desire for independence from Spain that prompted the first publication on the isthmus. Like many of the colonies that became independent from Spain, the printing press was introduced to Panama in the early 1820s by José María Goytía. Soon after, a four-page weekly publication named *La Miscelánea del Istmo* appeared, making it the first newspaper printed in Panama. After Panama's independence from Spain, other publications were in circulation. These included *La Gaceta de Panamá* (1830–1831), *La Unión* (1830), *El Istmeño* (1831), *El Constitucional del Istmo* (1831), *Comercio Libre* (1833–1834), *El Vigía del Istmo* (1834), *El Constitucional del Istmo* (1835), and *Los Amigos del País* (1835–1841). While all were in circulation, all publications in the Spanish language faced the challenge of being regulated by Bogota, because, during that period, Panama was part of Colombia.

After Panama's independence from Colombia in 1903, the United States was granted full control over the radio waves in the country and prohibited Panamanians from conducting any radio broadcasting. With the absence of radio transmission, newspapers were important for the distribution of information on the isthmus. After independence from Colombia, the newspaper industry flourished and quickly became politically oriented. This political component of the newspaper industry continued to the point that nearing presidential elections, newspapers were clearly partisan, openly attacking opposing candidates, and few, if any, were actually making an effort to be objective. This practice is not surprising, because many newspapers had come into existence before presidential elections to promote a specific candidate, and most of these candidates were either owners or the main shareholders of the major newspapers at any given time, a practice that continued well into the 1960s.

From the end of the 1960s until the end of the 1980s, Panama's newspaper industry underwent some of its most trying times because of its military regimes. Omar Torrijos, Rúben Darío Paredes del Río, and Manuel Antonio Noriega were all able to control the newspaper industry to some extent. They achieved their purpose by buying shares or doing whatever was necessary to have this control, even having newspapers stop production if they refused to comply with the military's desires. Perhaps the most important development during this time was *La Prensa* newspaper (1980). *La Prensa* became one of the military regime's most important adversaries; there were so many threats to *La Prensa* that it was forced to shut down for almost two years and did not continue circulation until the early 1990s after Operation Just Cause.

As for newspapers written in the English language in Panama, the first was *The Panama Star* (1849), which provided information on steamships on Panama's Pacific Ocean. Because of disagreements among *The Panama Star* shareholders, a few years later *The Panama Herald* (1851) made its appearance, and almost two years later, *The Daily News* (1853) was in circulation on the isthmus. In 1854, *The Panama Star* and *The Panama Herald* merged to become *The Star and Herald*, which remained in existence as one of the major sources of news for the English-speaking population in Panama until 1987. In more recent years, local and international news in the English language have been provided by *The Panama Post*, *The Bocas Breeze*, *The Bulletin*, *The Isthmian*, and *The Panama News*.

La Estrella de Panamá (1953) and *El Panamá América* (1927), which came into existence through the English-language newspapers *The Panama Star* and *The Panama American*, respectively, are not only among the first newspapers in the Spanish language to be published in Panama but also have become two of the leading newspapers in the country. Other major newspapers in Panama include *El Diario Universal de Panamá*, *La Crítica Libre*, *La Crónica*, *La Prensa*, *La República*, and *El Siglo*. Panama's major newspapers are all published in the capital city, and today they range from the sensational to the serious. In addition, online newspapers catering to local and international readers have become popular in Panama. They include the *Cybernews*, *Diario Net Online*, *Panactual*, the *Panama News*, and *El Tiempo de Panama*. Most of the major newspapers are also available on the Internet.

Because of their active role and growing numbers in Panama, there also have been significant contributions made to the printed media by the Chinese. There have been three major Chinese newspapers in Panama: *La República* (1930), *La Justicia* (1943), and *El Expresso* (1992); jointly they provide information on the local Chinese community in and around Panama City; local and international news specifically on China, Taiwan, Hong Kong, and Macao; and they recently have started distribution nationally.

Television

The development of television transmission on the isthmus is directly linked to the United States in the Canal Zone area. In 1954, the Southern Command Network Television (SCN-TV), the United States Arms Forces television station, became the first television station in the republic and transmitted until 1999, when the Torrijos-Carter treaties went into effect.

SCN-TV started out with channel 8 for coverage on the Pacific side of the isthmus, and later added channel 10 for coverage on the Atlantic side. It was created for information and entertainment purposes. It targeted United States soldiers, canal workers, and other Americans living in Panama; SCN-TV was also accessible to the general Panamanian public—basically to anybody who had a television. SCN-TV was not only the first television station in Panama to broadcast in black and white and later in color, but it was also the frontrunner for satellite transmission in the region.

Based on agreements from treaties between Panama and the United States, the United States controlled Panamanian airwaves, and Panama did not have the rights to television broadcasting. It was not until 1956, after extensive negotiations with the United States, that the Panamanian government was able to approve a decree that allowed for the establishment of national television stations on the isthmus.

On March 14, 1960, six years after SCN-TV had been broadcasting, the first Panamanian television station was inaugurated: RPC Televisión Canal 4. Two years later, in 1962, Televisora Nacional Canal 2 was transmitting, and by 1968 it became affiliated with the United States television station ABC, forming the Latin American Television International Network Organization (LATINO). Many other Latin American countries also joined (Handbook of Latin American Popular Culture 113). This affiliation enabled Televisora Nacional Canal 2 to raise its standards, making it the first Panamanian television station to transmit images in color.

In 1972 Canal Once was created, which later became RTVE Radio y *Televisión Educativa* (Educational Television), administered by Panamas Ministry of Education. The 1980s brought about Telemetro Canal 13, PanaVision del Istmo, and Canal 5; Canal 5 eventually became *FE-TV Fundacion para la Educación en Televisión* (Foundation for Education on Television) in the early 1990s.

Initially, live programming in Panama was limited to the news (twice a day), national lottery drawings (on Wednesdays and Sundays), some sports, and occasionally variety shows. Almost everything else that was transmitted was imported: soap operas mainly from Mexico and Venezuela, cartoons from Japan, and programs like *Dallas, Bonanza*, and the *A Team*, which were produced in the United States and dubbed in Spanish.

The end of the twentieth century brought with it even more variety in programming and the introduction of more sophisticated forms of television transmission and programming. The introduction of cable, satellite dishes, and fiber optics to Panama helped expose Panamanians to the rest of the world and further launch them into the wave of globalization.

Radio

Because of previous agreements, the United States not only monopolized the television station industry in Panama, but also the airwaves, which were primarily used for military purposes.

In the history of radio broadcasting in Panama, the first real attempt at radio transmissions by Panamanians occurred in July 1933, with transmissions from Radio Tembleque (also known as Radio Experimental). Initially Radio Tembleque had a capability of reaching approximately ten blocks but it quickly expanded its range. Because Radio Tembleque's broadcastings were unauthorized by the United States, they were deemed "illegal," and soon after the initial transmissions, the United States managed to stop the operation. However, Radio Tembleque already had a great number of listeners who manifested their unhappiness with the United States' intervention in the transmission and persuaded the Panamanian government to take action. After negotiations with the United States, Panama's government was able to grant a license for the operation of radio stations on the isthmus in 1934.

The first license was granted to Radio Miramar, but La Voz de Panamá emitted its first transmission on December 25, 1934, a few days before Radio Miramar, making it the first "legal" Panamanian radio station to broadcast in the country.

In 1941, SCN Radio (the Southern Command Network) transmitted in Panama, putting it among the first radio stations of United States military bases in the world. It was in operation until 1999. Initially, it started out in low frequency for military purposes and later expanded to include programming geared toward United States citizens living in Panama. Perhaps the most important moment for Panamanians was in 1989 during Operation Just Cause, when SCN Radio was able to provide Panamanians with information at a time when local information was limited.

From its beginnings, radio has played a key part in the distribution of news in Panama, and it was especially important for those who did not buy newspapers, could not afford to buy a television, or did not know how to read. Especially important over the years have been Radio Miramar, La Voz de Panamá, La CPR, Radio Programas Continental, Radio Mía, Red Panamericana, Radio Centroamericana, Radio Teatro Estrella, La Voz del Barú, La Voz de Aguadulce, and Ondas Chiricanas. In recent years, KW Continente and Radio Caracol have been added to the list. The most popular radio stations offer listeners alternate local and international news with sports, music, and radio talk shows.

Radio is still the largest means of communication. Local morning talk shows on the radio are popular, and most Panamanians have a favorite radio station. When walking in Panama at any given time, it is quite evident how the radio is an important part of day-to-day living. Most homes in Panama have at least one radio, and in the rural areas of Panama where keeping up on current events is sometimes difficult because of the lack of electricity, battery-powered radio is sometimes the only outlet to the rest of the world. From street vendors listening to their transistor radios, buses and taxis, business offices, and work sites, people are all tuned in to their particular station of choice. Today, Panama has more than ninety radio stations that provide a variety of programs including talk shows, soap operas, sarcastic political commentary, religious programs, sports coverage, and both local and international news. Like the diverse people in the country, Panamanians enjoy a variety of music, which is reflected in the type of music that radio stations play. Music ranges from traditional Panamanian music, salsa, merengue, and cumbia to jazz, reggae, rock, R&B, oldies, classical, and also include the latest hits from the United States. A list of the most popular Panamanian radio stations today includes la Exitosa, la Mega, Marbella Estereo, M.E.T.O. Stereo, Omega Stereo, Radio 10, Radio Hogar, RPC Radio, Super Q, and WAO 97.5.

Electronic Media

Like other countries in the region, Panama also has access to electronic media. Although the proportion of computers in Panamanian homes still remains significantly low compared with the United States, Internet access and use, especially by the younger generations, is available to Panamanians. One can get online at Internet cafés at a cost of as little as seventy-five cents per hour. Although the use of electronic media is still most prevalent in the capital city, it has also taken off throughout the country. This has changed the face of who is able to be part of the World Wide Web and become a part of the globalization trend. Internet cafés usually share their space with print shops, long-distance telephone calling centers, and cafeterias, and they are centrally located, close to universities, hotels, and highly transited areas. In the capital city, many internet cafés are open twenty-four hours a day, allowing even greater access to Panamanians. This form of media has influenced development in Panama and will continue to do so, as this all relates to globalization.

Magazines and Periodicals

The development of magazines and periodicals in Panama has been abundant from its inception. The first one to appear was *El Heraldo del Istmo* (1904), which was created for the promotion of literature but later included some articles on cultural aspects such as music and history. Over the years, many periodicals and magazines have appeared and disappeared mainly because of economic reasons, but one of the most important still in existence today is *Revista Lotería* (1941), which is funded by the state. *Revista Lotería* includes articles that cover diverse subjects and aspects of Panama's culture and life, including history, music, architecture, law, and the sciences.

Panama's volatile political situation at the end of the twentieth century is reflected in the content of periodicals and magazines; today, there are still magazines and periodicals dedicated to varied interests. Nevertheless, the number of periodicals and magazines promoting Panama as a vacation and retirement destination for United States citizens as well as real state opportunities is growing, reflecting once more Panama's reality as a crossroads of the world.

CINEMA

The film or movie industry in Panama has not made as great strides as other markets in the country, yet, it has not remained totally behind. It has and continues to be a struggling industry. Although Panama does not play a significant role in the production of film compared with other countries, it continues to work hard toward that goal. The country has a made a name for itself as the site of many documentaries, movies, and, recently, a reality television show.

As a place of transit, Panama's citizens were among the first in the region to experience film at the beginning of the twentieth century. Shortly after independence from Colombia, many venues for watching films opened in the major cities of the new republic, but the films were imported from other places. It was not until the 1940s that filming by Panamanians really began. The major force behind this development was Ladislao Sosa, who had studied in Mexico and brought his ideas back to Panama. Nevertheless, it is Carlos Luis Nieto's 1946 film *Al calor de mi bohío* (At the Heat of my Bohío) that is considered the start of filmmaking in Panama.

The next major moment in filmmaking in Panama was the creation of the state supported company GECU *Grupo Experimental de Cine Universitario* (Experimental University Cinema Group) in the 1970s. The films produced during this time focused mainly on the treaties between Panama and the United States, as the Canal was the burning topic of the decade. The same can be said for the 1990s, with the major topic of interest being the invasion of Panama by the United States.

After the invasion and going into the new millennium, CIMAS, the *Centro de Imágenes y Sonidos* (Images and Sound Center) was created. Today, several film festivals have been organized as well as Cine clubs. To date, one of the most important steps for this industry has been the passing of *La Ley de Cine* (Cinematographic and Audiovisual Promotion Law) in 2007, which states that cinematography plays a key part in the formation of a national identity and will be supported by the state.

Documentaries on the Panama Canal are perhaps the most numerous, ranging from everything from its engineering to the historical and cultural realities of its existence. Other aspects of Panama's history have also appeared on film. One of the most famous is *The Panama Deception* (1992), about the 1989 United States invasion of Panama, which won the 1992 Academy Award for Best Documentary Feature.

A couple of movies have had Panama as its location. One of the most recent is *The Tailor of Panama* (2001), about a tailor living in Panama who becomes a British spy. Recently, segments of the latest James Bond movie were filmed in the colonial neighborhood called Casco Viejo in Panama City and in the province of Colón.

Although the major actors of these films are not Panamanian, one Panamanian has managed to put Panama on the map in the cinema industry: Panama's current minister of tourism, Rubén Blades. In addition to being one of Latin America's most outstanding salsa singers and composers as well as Grammy and Latin Grammy winner from the early 1980s, he has also appeared in several Hollywood films. Rubén Blades's recent appearances include *All the Pretty Horses* (2000), *Assassination Tango* (2003), *Imagining Argentina* (2003), *Once Upon a Time in Mexico* (2003), *Secuestro Express* (2005), and *Grandpa* (2008).

Panamanians enjoy going to the movies, and the number of movie theaters has increased. Panama City has at least eight movie theaters, several in the mall areas as well as in the cities of Colón, Chitré, Chorrera, and David. Most of the featured films are the same ones that are playing in the United States, and occasionally foreign films will play at these venues. Because these films are in English, they are usually subtitled or dubbed in Spanish.

The Republic of Panama has also been the site for two episodes of the reality show *Survivor*, with the seasons *Survivor: Exile Island* and *Survivor: All-Star* both filmed on Panama's Pearl Islands.

6

Architecture and Housing

ARCHITECTURE

As a result of the country's unique and rich history, from its indigenous people to the *conquistadors* to the twentieth century, the influences of the many changes the isthmus has undergone are reflected and chronicled in its architecture and architectural styles. One can only marvel at the architectural variety found in the Republic of Panama.

We can start our journey of Panama's architecture by first examining the dwellings of the native people, which technically were the first forms of architecture in the area. Many important structures from the colonial period are still standing; among them are a series of buildings called *Panamá la Vieja* (Old Panama).

When Panama City was attacked by buccaneers and underwent an extensive fire, the city was rebuilt in a new location known today as *Casco Viejo* or *Casco Antiguo* (Old City). It is a beautiful Spanish-style colonial city with buildings that are currently being restored. In addition, Panama recently acquired *Áreas Revertidas* (the former Canal Zone area), with structures that range from commercial (banks and restaurants) to residential. In terms of more modern architecture, there are the *Puente Centenario* and modern high-rise condominiums featuring the latest in architectural design. Panama has an impressive variety of architectural styles.

Unlike other areas of the Americas, where we see monumental expression of precolonial architecture by natives, Panama does not have this. Regarding structures from the colonial period, except for the *Casco Antiguo* area, very little has been preserved. When one explores modern architecture in Panama, specifically in Panama City, it is seen that there are many structures that are among the most impressive and extraordinary in the region. Through architecture, one is able to see and appreciate the many changes and transformations Panama has undergone, exposing its rich history. Modern structures that display the latest techniques and features of architectural design stand in sharp contrast to ruins that date back to colonial times. Modern high-rise condominiums, as well as recently acquired structures from the former Canal Zone, come together to give us yet another view of Panama's richness.

Before Discovery

When the *conquistadores* arrived in the area that would later become Panama, there was no architecture to speak of. Native Indians in the region lived in functional dwellings, the primary purpose of which was to provide shelter. There was no known distinctive style. Most of the information that we have today on the way these first inhabitants lived is from information provided by Gonzalo Fernández de Oviedo y Valdés in his *Historia General y Natural de las Indias* (General and Natural History of the Indies). Based on what we know about the dwellings of Panama's native Indians in the past and present, it is evident that very little has changed.

There are three major indigenous groups in the country: the Guaymí (Ngobe-Bugle), Kuna, and Choco (Embere-Wounaan) Indians; and the three major types of indigenous dwellings that are represented in the Republic of Panama are theirs. The Guaymí Indians, who are generally located in the provinces of Chiriquí, Bocas del Toro, and Veraguas, have two types of dwellings. Most of the year they live in circular, dirt-floor dwellings; the walls are made of wooden frames, covered with mud and livestock manure, and have roofs made of palm trees. Many Guaymí Indians also have a second dwelling located on the banks of rivers, where they live during the summer months to be able to do their fishing. A distinctive characteristic of the Guaymí Indians is that in their communities, their dwellings are not close to one another—their communities are dispersed throughout the land.

In contrast to the Guaymí Indians' huts, the Kuna huts are rectangular, and the major support of the structure is in the center. The walls are made of *caña blanca*, which is a kind of cane, and the roof is made of palm tree leaves. The huts are divided into two spaces: one large living space that is also used for sleeping, and another smaller space usually located in the back that is used as a kitchen, eating area, and warehouse. Also, while the Guaymí Indians' two types of dwellings are based on climate and the need for food, the Kunas' two dwellings are structurally the same, but their physical distribution varies by location, which is either the San Blas Islands or the coastal mainland. Although in both cases Kuna Indian huts are constructed in close proximity to one another, on the San Blas Islands huts seem to be built randomly, and on the coastal mainland they are constructed in a more orderly fashion.

The Choco Indians are a fishing community and live in square dwellings that are elevated from the ground because they live at the banks of rivers, lakes, and the ocean. Their dwellings are not located in close proximity but are rather scattered. The living space in these dwellings consists of one large area with no walls, constructed on poles, and like the dwellings of the Guaymí and the Kuna Indians, the roof is also made of palm tree leaves. What has been described for the Guaymí, Kuna, and Chocoe Indians basically is the way they have lived since the Spaniards came to the region more than 500 years ago.

Colonization

After colonization, Spaniards started settlements in the New World and in-fluenced the existing culture in many different ways, including architecture. They first started by building structures for practical use and day-to-day living and later built buildings for official and religious purposes. Once Panama became a major route to transport people and goods via the *Camino Real* (Royal Road), it also became necessary to build forts. Today, not much is left of the initial years of the *conquista*. Most of the evidence of those early years is in the form of ruins.

Today, Panama still has many different examples of colonial architecture; some are in good condition, but most have not been maintained or preserved. Nevertheless, efforts are being made to correct this problem. Panama has had well over a decade of political stabilization, and for this reason the Panamanian government has been able to begin to focus efforts on conducting restoration projects. Although for many structures this effort has begun too late, Panama still has some valuable examples of the colonial period, which can be found on the Pacific coast and around Panama City.

Casonas

Dating back to structures from the colonial period, the Republic of Panama has several large houses called *Casonas*, many of which are still in use today. Most are made of thick walls and have beautiful balconies, central courtyards, or gardens; they also have a vestibule that leads to a receiving area and a patio, which, in turn, allows access to the bedrooms on the second floor. The first and second floors of the house are constructed around the patio. Although Panama City has many *Casonas*, some of the most beautiful are in *Villa de los Santos* in the city of David, Chiriquí. Today, these *Casonas* still have people living in them. In Panama City, many *Casonas* are rental properties divided into multiple apartments.

Military Structures

In addition to the *Casonas*, the Spaniards built several military structures for protection during the colonial period. Initially, fortresses were constructed by Spaniards for protection against attacks from Indians, blacks, and foreigners who wanted to take over the areas they had "conquered." Although not many of these fortresses remain, in addition to Panama City and Portobelo, there are some ruins in Chepo, Isla de Taboga, and Darién.

Because of the *Camino Real*, most of Panama's major forts were in Panama City and Portobelo. One of the most important is Fort San Lorenzo, which was built on a high mountain at the mouth of the Chagres River. The exact date of the construction of the San Lorenzo Fort is unclear, but it was ordered to be built sometime toward the end of the sixteenth century and underwent numerous attacks. As pirates vandalized the *Camino Real*, the route for transporting gold that came from Peru and crossed the isthmus on its way to Spain, Fort San Lorenzo was also affected. In 1596, Francis Drake set the fort on fire, and in 1761, the fort was moved and rebuilt. By the time Panama became part of Colombia, it was used as a prison. It had deteriorated over the years and has been recently renovated as a tourist site, best known for its original canons.

In the mid-1600s, after Panama City was moved to its second location below the Ancon Hill, fortresses were constructed to give the new city protection. Unfortunately, most of it was demolished in the 1850s, but today we can still see some fragments of walls and arches and in some cases significant pieces of the original structure. An example is *Las Bóvedas* (The Dungeon), which literally means dungeon, also known as *Plaza de Francia*. *Las Bóvedas* was part of a fortress: it was a torture chamber and an underground prison. Today, it is a French restaurant and has two art galleries that are all distinct and have colonial charm.

On the Atlantic coast, Portobelo is the most important site when it comes to colonial architecture. Portobelo has different examples of colonial structures, one of which is the customs building. The customs building was built in a bay close to Portobelo's banks in the early 1630s to allow access to Portobelo both by land and by sea. Unfortunately, this structure was damaged by an earthquake in 1882, but there is still evidence of its existence. In addition, there is the *Real Aduana de Portobelo* (customs house), where all of the gold and silver was counted. It has been restored and is now a museum.

In Portobelo, the main fort is San Felipe, also known as *Todo Fierro* (iron fort). It is documented that construction of the San Felipe Fort started sometime in the last decade of the 1500s and that ruins existed until 1909, when it became a quarry. The United States used the stones from the fort for the construction of the *Gatún* (Atlantic coast) portion of the Canal.

In Portobelo, we also find the San Jerónimo Castle. Its construction was started in the mid-1600s; at one point it was attacked by pirates, but toward the middle of the eighteenth century it was restored. In addition, there is also the *Santiago de la Glória* castle, also known as *Santiago del Príncipe*. The construction started at the end of the 1500s, and like the *Castillo de San Jerónimo*, it was also attacked by pirates. Although it was restored in the mid-eighteenth century, only its ruins are left today. Other castles were *Castillo de San Cristóbal, Castillo de San Fernando, San Fernandito, Fuerte de Triana,* and *Fuerte El Perú.*

Religious Structures

Panama has its fair share of religious structures. Colonization in the region was motivated in part and justified by the need to "save" and convert the people on the American continent. Thus, Panama has several religious structures that represent this period.

Based on the importance of its location during the colonial period, several religious structures existed in Portobelo, including *La Iglesia Mayor* and *El Convento de la Merced*. Of these structures, only ruins and some walls are still standing today. Still in use today, the most famous church in Portobelo is the *Iglesia San Felipe*, where the *Cristo Negro* (Black Christ), also known as the *Nazareno*, is housed. San Felipe was inaugurated in 1814 and is said to be the last building constructed in Portobelo by Spain. Behind the *Iglesia San Felipe* is *La Iglesia San Juan de Dios*, which was a hospital but is now a small museum connected to the San Felipe Church.

One of the most important religious structures during the colonial period in the region that would later become Panama was *La Catedral* (the Cathedral) in *Panamá la Vieja* (Old Panama). This cathedral was originally constructed of straw in 1519 and its masonry was inaugurated in 1626. It had three floors and six bells. It suffered two major tragedies: The first was a fire in 1644 and the second was an assault by buccaneers in 1671, when they attacked and looted the area now known as *Panamá la Vieja*. After these incidents, the bells and all the materials that could be reused were taken to the new location of Panama City. Because of the lack of money, this second cathedral was originally constructed of wood. From 1676 to 1749, the plan of the cathedral changed several times to what we have today. In the first part of the 1900s, the cathedral underwent several restorations that have changed its original appearance. Although very little of the original structure of the cathedral is standing, today this structure has come to represent *Panamá la Vieja*.

In the second site of Panama City in the San Felipe District there is the San José Church in the area known as *El Casco Viejo* or *Casco Antiguo*. The San José Church is a small building that houses the famous *Altar de Oro* (Golden Altar). The church was constructed between 1671 and 1677 and remodeled in the nineteenth century. The *Altar de Oro* was made in a baroque style, with carved mahogany and gilded with golden filigree; it was initially in a church in *Panamá la Vieja*. When *Panamá la Vieja* was attacked and destroyed by the English pirate Henry Morgan, the altar was painted black to disguise it. Soon after the attack, it was moved to its present location.

In this area of Panama City, one finds much colonial baroque architecture, such as the *San Francisco de Asis* church. A mixture of colonial and neoclassical styles, the *Iglesia de la Catedral* was built sometime between the seventeenth and eighteenth centuries, and after it was damaged in an earthquake, it was reconstructed in the nineteenth century. La Merced Church and Santa Ana Church are also beautiful buildings depicting the colonial era.

Another important structure in Panama City built during colonial times was the Santo Domingo Church. By the 1670s, there were both a convent and a church with the name of Santo Domingo. At the time of its construction, the Santo Domingo Cathedral was one of the largest and most magnificent church structures in Panama. Constructed by Dominican monks, its woodwork was destroyed by a fire in 1756 and was never rebuilt. Of all the features in the Santo Domingo Church, the most important structural piece is the *Arco Chato* (Flat Arch). The *Arco Chato* has gotten a lot of attention because it has been standing for over 300 years; every other area of the structure was damaged except this one. The fact that the *Arco Chato* was standing for so long was an indication that Panama was not an earthquake zone, and this was one of the factors that influenced the building of the Panama Canal. However, on November 7, 2003, after the celebrations of Panama's one hundred years of independence, the arch collapsed. It is not clear exactly why the *Arco Chato* collapsed, but it has been attributed to the increase of bus traffic to the area, mainly bringing tourists to the site, and to the vibrations of the celebrations that year in the area for the centennial coupled with its deteriorating condition.

With its baroque architecture, the San Francisco de la Montaña Church was founded in the early 1720s in the province of Veraguas and was declared a national historical monument in 1937. It is still standing today, but because it has gone through several restorations, very little of its original details remain. The San Anastasio Church in the province of Los Santos was also declared a national monument in the 1930s and underwent several stages of reconstruction in the eighteenth century. The San Anastasio Church houses several colonial baroque carved altars. The Santo Domingo de Guzman Church in Parita in the province of Herrera is of importance not so much for its architecture but for what it contains. Its construction dates back to the seventeenth century, and it has a bell tower that hangs over its front door.

Throughout the republic, many churches have had major reconstructions. In the province of Veraguas, for example, the Natá Church, which was one of the richest churches in the New World, has undergone renovations. Also, the San Atanasio Church in the province of Los Santos has undergone several stages of reconstruction. Many other colonial churches in Panama that date back to the colonial period have been restored, but the jobs have been of poor quality, and many of these structures have lost not only their original importance but also their charm and original beauty.

Architecture after Independence from Spain

After independence from Spain, the former colonies started looking away from Spain and to France and England for new inspiration as they designed and built, and Panama was no exception. After Panama received its independence from Spain and became part of Colombia, the region underwent yet another stage, as is evidenced in its architecture. Once Panama became part of Colombia, many new and exciting things started happening on the isthmus. Transformation took place in the form of new constructions, the most important being the railroad and the first attempt at the construction of a canal in Panama in 1881 by the French. In 1855, during the period that Panama was part of Colombia, the Railroad Station Terminal that offered transportation between Panama on the Pacific and Colón on the Atlantic side was first built and was rebuilt several times after that.

The construction of the Canal by the French brought hundreds of Frenchmen to Panama, so it was inevitable for Panama to be influenced by them. Perhaps the influence of the French in the architecture is most noticeable in the buildings that were constructed as living quarters in the provinces of Panama and Colón. These living quarters were made of wood, were three to four stories high, had wide balconies that went out to the length of the sidewalks, and although only a few have been maintained, they give us an accurate picture of what it was like at that time.

The most important and famous building that captured the French influence is the *Gran Hotel*. The *Gran Hotel* is a French colonial–style building built in 1875. In 1881, the French bought the building and used it as their Canal Headquarters. When Americans took over the construction of the Canal the building became theirs, and once it was returned to the Panamanian government, it was restored and opened in 1997 as the Panama Canal Museum.

After the French influence, Panama had a burst of neoclassical influence in its architecture. This style in architecture arrived in Panama toward the beginning of the twentieth century, as it did in the rest of the region. Toward the end of the period that Panama was part of Colombia—that is, the turn of the century—many important government buildings were constructed. The many architectural styles (Spanish, French, and Italian)—mostly neoclassical—are clustered in the *Casco Antiguo* (*Casco Viejo*), which today is the District of San Felipe. *El Palacio Municipal* (the Municipal Palace), *El Palacio de Gobierno y Justicia* (the Government Palace), and *La Corte Suprema de Justicia* (the Supreme Court) reflect these styles.

Although Panama seems to have gone through the neoclassical phase, as evidenced by its many constructions, once Panama was established as an independent nation, the architecture of the major government buildings that were constructed was more modern and practical, leaving very little in terms of originality.

Independence from Colombia

In 1903, when Panama became an independent nation after separation from Colombia, much needed to be done in the country, as buildings for the many segments of life were needed. Many of these new constructions became the first of their kind in the country.

During the first decade of independence, several schools were built in Panama City. Among the most important were the *Artes y Oficios* and the famous *Instituto Nacional*. Also during that time, both the *Palacio de Gobierno* and the National Theater, which were built in a neoclassical style, were constructed. Special attention was given to the theater, because it was clear that it was going to be the only one of its kind for a while.

During this early period of independence, construction was also taking place in other parts of the country to help with the needs of public life. Government offices and palaces, police headquaters, as well as schools were built in the various provinces of Bocas del Toro, Chiriquí, Coclé, Colón, and Los Santos. This construction impacted the entire Republic of Panama.

The Pacific side railroad station terminal, originally built in 1855 and rebuilt several times thereafter, had its last major work done in 1913. Over the years, changes were made, and by 1976 it opened as the *El Museo del Hombre Panameño* (the Museum of the Panamanian Man). After many years of renovation, it reopened in 2000 as *El Museo Antropológico Reina Torres de Araúz*, Panama's Anthropology Museum.

Religious structures were also constructed during this period. In addition to the customary Catholic churches and cathedrals that one finds in Latin America built during colonial times, Panama has several other impressive religious structures representing many faiths. The Methodist, Baptist, Episcopal, and Anglican Churches constructed on the Atlantic and Pacific sides of the isthmus were built mostly after work on the railroad and Canal was initiated for Americans and West Indians who came to Panama. Founded in the 1850s for the British shipping community and the American railroad workers, the Anglican Christ Church by the Sea in the province of Colón is among the most important in the country and is said to be the second-oldest structure of its kind in Latin America.

Perhaps the most impressive non-Catholic structure in Panama is the Bahá'í House of Worship, which is one of only eight in the world. Its construction began in 1967, and it was dedicated in 1972. The Bahá'í House of Worship is a domed structure that overlooks Panama City. Made of local stones with intricate patterns and tile work, this building is truly unique. In August 2008, the Mormon Temple, the third in the region, was inaugurated in Panama City.

Today, Panama City is one of the most modern cities in Latin America. Approximately one-third of all Panamanians live in or around Panama City. Panama's *Area Bancaria*, which is the financial district, is one of the largest and most important in the region. Panama also has state-of-the-art hotels, casinos, and restaurants.

To date, one of the government's most successful projects in an attempt to preserve the past is *Mi Pueblito* (my little town). It consists of replicas of architectural styles of three major cultures in Panama: West Indian, Spanish, and Native Indian. The West Indian and Spanish villages consist of several life-sized structures that surround an open courtyard. The West Indian village provides a vivid idea of the dwellings of Caribbean workers and their families during the period of the construction of the Panama Canal. It also includes a replica of the Christian Mission Church, founded in 1910. The original structure still exists today and serves as the *Museo Afro-Antillano de Panamá* (the West Indian Museum of Panama).

The Spanish village has replicas of different types of colonial-style structures, which include churches and classrooms. Similarly, the Native Indian village has life-sized replicas of different huts that depict the dwellings and meeting places of the principal indigenous groups in the country. Many of the buildings in *Mi Pueblito* are museums, restaurants, and gift and souvenir shops.

December 1999 marked the final turnover of the Canal and the Canal Zone to the Panamanian people. Panamanians received all of the former military bases that were controlled and administered by the United States government. Most of the buildings received were either sold or rented. Some were used by the private sector, while others were converted into government offices. A number of the original military structures remained practically intact; however, many vacant land areas became prime real estate property. New housing developments and commercial buildings were constructed. The Albrook Mall and the Albrook Terminal are excellent examples of how the acquired areas have been used.

HOUSING

Homes in Panama vary extensively depending on if they are in an urban or rural location. Rural homes are small and have one or two rooms, walls are generally made of sugarcane stalk or branches held together with mud, and roofs are made of palm branches. Homes in the cities are mostly one story made of cement blocks, with tile or tin roofs. These houses can be in a community similar to housing developments in the United States or just on parcels of land. They are often surrounded by elaborate fences also made out of cement with metal decorations for privacy. Gardens are usually very small. In the major cities as well as along the major highways, the poor live in tenement buildings or shacks generally made of wood or tin. On the other hand, the wealthy live in large luxury homes and apartments. With the new boom in home and apartment construction, standards are rising and are more like those in the United States.

In addition to the modern high-rise condominiums and commercial buildings in Panama, the *Puente Centenario* (Centennial Bridge), inaugurated in 2004, is one of Panama's most modern and finest architectural structures. This bridge was built to share the traffic on the *Puente de las Américas* (Bridge of the Americas), also known as the Thatcher Ferry Bridge. The *Puente de las Américas* was built between 1958 and 1962 to replace the ferry that connected the Pan-American Highway, the connecting highway between North America and South America, thus bridging the gap created during the construction of the Panama Canal. Another important structure that dates back to 1935 is the Madden Dam. It controls the Chagres River waters and today is one of the major sources for hydroelectric power.

The Canal

By far the most important and impressive structure in the country is the Panama Canal. One of the marvels of modern engineering and considered by some to be the "eighth wonder of the world," the Panama Canal was completed on August 15, 1914. The Canal is essential for cutting time and distance for globetrotters and is essential for commerce not only in Latin America but in the entire world.

The Canal runs from the Atlantic to the Pacific Oceans, has seventeen artificial lakes, several channels, and three sets of locks: Miraflores, Gatún, and Pedro Miguel. The Gatún Lake is one of the largest manmade lakes in the world. The Canal is approximately 51 miles long, and each lock is

110 feet wide by 1,000 feet long. Due to the increase in the size of vessels, Panama is trying to keep up with the demands of the changing world, and on October 22, 2006, legislation for its expansion was passed. Work started on September 3, 2007, and the renovated Panama Canal is scheduled for August 15, 2014, the centennial of its opening.

7

Visual and Performing Arts

As CITIZENS OF a rich and changing country, Panamanians enjoy many forms of visual art—it is literally a part of Panamanian everyday life. From the intricate paintings and decorations on buses to wood carvings, pottery, and *mola* hand-sewn art to traditional music and dance performances in schools and festivals across the isthmus, it is quite clear that art in all its dimensions is an important part of life for Panamanians.

VISUAL ART AND CRAFTS

Popular Art

To survey visual art in this nation would seem like nothing is spared. Popular art can be found throughout the country; it is always on public display. One of the most common and distinct forms of popular art in Panama can be found on buses in the cities of Panama and Colón. These buses are called *Diablos Rojos* (Red Devil), and structurally they are similar to school buses in the United States. The *Diablos Rojos* are painted and decorated in vivid colors and usually have portraits of local and international contemporary celebrities. Buses are generally given names of women, and a practice is to have horoscope signs painted on the windows and proverbs printed on the bumpers. It is not unusual to hear music blasting from the buses with the latest hits, and in addition, some buses even display party lights, making a ride in the *Diablos Rojos* an unforgettable experience. These buses are used by locals as public transportation. In addition to the art that is displayed on the buses throughout the streets of Panama, there are several murals on public display, both as advertisements and commissioned work.

Crafts in Panama

Like most countries in Latin America, Panamanian crafts include a variety of items that range from woodcarvings to pottery and handwoven baskets to hats and masks. Some of the more unique Panamanian arts and crafts include miniature tropical animal figurine sculptures made by the Wounaan and Embere tribes from the tagua nut. The tagua nut is the seed of the tagua palm tree; it is white and often compared to ivory. Woven baskets made by the Embere from the chunga palm, arm bracelets called *chaquiras* made of beads by women from Coclé, and chacaras, which are bags made by the Ngobe-Bugle tribe from pineapple plants, are also very popular. In addition, book-ends and figures depicting animals, mangers, national sites, and heroes made of soapstone are also popular. The most distinctive handmade craft associated with Panama is the famous *mola*, made by the Kuna Indians.

Molas, which are used in the back and front of Kuna Indian women's blouses, are colorful and meticulously handstitched cloth appliqué panels. The finer the stitch, the more valuable the *mola* is. *Molas* are made of several layers (between two and seven) of brightly colored fabric. Traditionally, *mola* designs were animal shapes, usually fish and birds, or abstract shapes. Today, traditional shapes are still popular but new designs have appeared. Designs are endless and can be custom-made. Detailed maps of Panama, as well as flags, mostly of the United States and Panama, have become increasingly popular among tourists. In recent years, this indigenous art has been incorporated into modern-day Panama; we find *molas* on clothes, shoes, kitchen items (kitchen towels, potholders), pillows, and handbags. The *mola* is perhaps Panama's best example of how traditional Panamanian art has made its way into mainstream contemporary life. The use of *mola* design possibilities on decorations, clothing, and wall design is infinite.

Every year the *Ministerio Panameño de Comercio e Industria* (Panamanian Ministry of Commerce and Industry) sponsors the *Feria Nacional de Artesanía* (National Fair of Crafts) in the ATLAPA (Atlantic and Pacific Convention Center) in Panama City. Different Panamanian crafts are represented at the event, and prizes are awarded to the best artisans in several categories.

In addition to the *Mercados Artesanales* (artisan markets), where Panamanian crafts are sold by the native craftsmen themselves or a member of their family, the crafts are also mass-produced. It is not unusual to find craft items at department stores, major supermarkets, or even on the Internet. Panamanians are putting technology to good use, and sales have become global. What would be considered art in the traditional sense did not appear in Panama until the beginning of the twentieth century.

Painters in Panama

Because of Panama's location as a place of transit in the nineteenth century, many traveling artists visited Panama. These artists were successful at painting important moments in the country, most the construction of the railroad company in the mid-1900s and the canal by the French in the 1880s.

After these transient painters, we find a number of works by national portrait painters that in a way became the first Panamanian national art. Among the most outstanding artists were the Colombian-born Epifanio Garay (1849–1903) and Sebastián Villalaz (1879–1919), who also painted Panama's first Coat of Arms, created by his brother, Nicanor Villalaz.

From the end of the nineteenth century to the beginning of the twentieth century, the development of an artistic tradition in Panama continued to be very slow, with a few artists emerging after independence from Colombia in 1903. During this time, the best paintings by a Panamanian artist were murals by Roberto Lewis (1874–1949). Panama's most famous painter, he was an educator and ended up having great influence over artists who would eventually become part of the first generation of Panamanian painters. Nevertheless, Manuel Encarnación Amador (1869–1952), Panamanian President Manuel Amador Guerrero's son, also made a name for himself in the artistic world during that time.

Manuel Encarnación Amador traveled extensively doing diplomatic work and took advantage of his many locations to study painting. The two most important places where Manuel Encarnación Amador studied were Germany and New York. He is best known for his outstanding oil paintings, especially of human figures and landscapes. His importance in Panama's history lies in having designed Panama's national flag in 1908.

Roberto Lewis studied in France and won many national and international prizes for his artistic work. While in Paris, he created works on canvas, which he later brought to Panama. In 1913, he became founder and the first director of the *Academia Nacional de Pintura* (National Academy of Painting), which was Panama's first art academy. He was commissioned to paint the official portraits of Panamanian leaders and presidents. His most celebrated works of art are displayed at the Presidential Palace, the Juan Demóstenes Arosemena School, and in Panama's National Theater. One of the most important aspects of his landscape painting was the tamarind tree. His 1942 painting "Tamarindos" (Tamarind Trees) is an excellent example of his work.

Of Roberto Lewis's students, the best known were Humberto Ivaldi and Juan Manuel Cedeño; they went on to become some of the best artists in

Panama and part of what has become the First Generation of Panamanian painters. Like their teacher, they both focused on painting portraits and had an academic approach to painting, one in tune with European standards. They later became the teachers of the following generation.

Humberto Ivaldi was born in Panama City (1909–1947). He first studied with Roberto Lewis and later continued his studies at the Bellas Artes de San Fernando Academy in Spain. Ivaldi is considered Panama's finest landscape painter. Along with Roberto Lewis, Humberto Ivaldi was active in the National Academy of Painting and was responsible for educating the next generation of artists, which included Manuel Cedeño, Ciro Obuder, Eudoro Silvera, Juan Bautista Jeanine, Isaac Benítez, and Alfredo Sinclair.

After Roberto Lewis and Humberto Ivaldi, the majority of Panama's leading painters started their painting foundation by studying under them at the National Academy of Painting. Nevertheless, their art differs a great deal, due to the fact that in addition to studding in Panama, many Panamanian artists had the opportunity to travel to different countries and study abroad at different institutions under some of the worlds most respected artists, and this exposure in many cases had a great impact on their work.

Juan Manuel Cedeño (1914–1999) was born in the province of Los Santos and started his artistic career as a student under Roberto Lewis at the National Academy of Painting. Cedeño earned a B.A. degree from the Chicago Institute of Art and also studied in Mexico City at the Polytechnic Institute under Diego Rivera. He went on to become the director of Panama's Academy of Painting and a professor of drawing and painting at Panama University.

After Roberto Lewis passed away, Cedeño continued his work of painting the official portraits of Panamanian presidents. He was commissioned to retouch Lewis's paintings on the ceiling and foyer of the National Theater. In addition to portraits, Cedeño also painted beautiful rustic, folkloric, historic, and religious scenes; much of his inspiration came from the province of Los Santos, and he was proud to be from that region. He worked in charcoal, tempera, oil, and watercolor.

Another well-known painter and art teacher of this first generation is Rubén Villaláz Solís (1897–1994). Unlike Cedeño and Ivaldi, he did not study under Lewis. He was born in Los Santos. He studied art at the Academia San Carlos and the Escuela Normal Superior in México City and also in Rome, and this European influence is noticeable in his work. He served as director of the Escuela Nacional de Artes Plásticas for some years and is best known for his paintings of rural areas, especially his beautiful *campesino* scenes, as well as for his nude torsos of women from the countryside.

In addition to Juan Manuel Cedeño and Rubén Villaláz Solís, Isaac Leonardo Benítez, Juan Bautista Jeanine, Ciro Oduber, and Eudoro Silvera are also considered first-generation painters. Isaac Leonardo Benítez (1927–1968) studied under Humberto Ivaldi, and he was relatively an unknown painter when he had the opportunity to go to the Florentina Academy of Fine Arts in Italy to study. In 1947, he was given the Ivaldi Award. Juan Bautista Jeanine (1922–1982) studied sculpting at the Artes y Oficio High School in Panama City and had some training with Lewis and Ivaldi. He also studied in Argentina. Jeanine is best known for his murals on buildings all over the republic. Ciro Oduber (1921–2000) began his artistic studies with Lewis and continued with Ivaldi. He traveled to Argentina and was enrolled at the Escuela Superior de Bellas Artes Ernesto de Cárcova. He was best known for his geometric lines in murals and his drawings of animals and human beings and also for his many images of the crucifixion. Eudoro Silvera, who was from the province of Chiriquí (1917–?), started his art studies in the Escuela Nacional de Pintura and then continued his studies at the Cooper Union in New York City. He is best known for his drawings and caricatures. Alfredo Sinclair Ballesteros (1915–?) was Humberto Ivaldi and Roberto Lewis's student at the National School of Painting. He later traveled to Argentina and studied at the Escuela Superior de Bellas Artes Ernesto de la Cárcova. At that time, Argentina was the key location for abstract painting in Latin America. Ballesteros won numerous awards for his work, and many of his pieces are displayed in key locations, such as the Museum of Modern Art in New York City and the *Instituto Nacional de Bellas Artes* in Mexico. Ballesteros's importance lies in the fact that he is the first Panamanian to make use of abstract expressionism, a technique that many Panamanians did not understand.

Moving toward the middle of the twentieth century, a new group of Panamanian artists emerged. Most of these artists were born between the 1920s and 1930s and became internationally known, and most have had major exhibits at the headquarters of the Organization of American States in Washington, DC. The most famous include Pablo Runyan, Guillermo Trujillo, Manuel Chang Neto, Adriano Herrerabarría, Desiderio Sánchez, Julio Zachrisson, and Alberto Dutary. Most of these artists had the opportunity to study and work in Spain and Mexico, which had a significant impact on their work.

Guillermo Trujillo (1927–?) is from the province of Chiriquí. He is considered to be one of Panama's most exceptional artists, mostly due to his fame outside Panama. He studied painting in Madrid, Spain, and held expositions in France, Germany, Spain, and the United States. In 1981, he founded the Taller de Cerámica Las Guabas and served as its director until 1984. Guillermo Trujillo tried many artistic forms, but he is best known for his paintings of Panama before colonization. His art expresses a strong political and social satire. Manuel Chong Neto (1927–?) was born in Panama City and studied under Cedeño and later at the Academia de San Carlos de la Universidad Nacional Autónoma de México in Mexico. He concentrated on the human shape, and he is best known for his *gordas*, voluptuous figures of women who pose both with and without clothes. Adriano Herrerabarría (1928–?) studied in Mexico and is best known for his murals and his use of realism and later surrealism in his work. He was instrumental in the development of art schools in the interior of the country. Another influential artist is Desiderio Sánchez (1930–?), from Bocas del Toro, who focused on marine themes.

A significant number of Panama's artists relocated to Spain. Among the most important are Pablo Runyan Kelting (1925–2002), Ciro Oduber (1921–?), Julio Zachrisson (1930–?), and Alberto Dutary (1932–?).

Pablo Runyan Kelting (1925–2002) was born in Panama and lived there until he was about twenty years old. He then lived in New York City, traveled the world, and finally settled in Spain. Although he produced some literature and did some work in film and theater, by the 1970s he focused exclusively on painting. He is an important figure because he introduced surrealism to painting, although many argue that he did not stay long enough in Panama to have a lasting impact on Panama's artistic world.

Ciro Oduber is best known for his use of geometric forms in his paintings. In addition to being a painter, Julio Zachrisson is known for using other techniques, including lithography on aluminum plaques. Alberto Dutary (1932–1998) was born in Panama City. He initiated his artistic studies at the Escuela Nacional de Artes Plasticas and later went to Madrid to the Academia San Fernando and the Escuela de Artes Gráficas. He was instrumental in the teaching and development of art in Panama.

Other exceptional artists include Antonio Alvarado (1938–?); Luis Aguilar Ponce of Panama City (1943–?); Rogelio Pretto (1944–?), from the province of Colón, famous for his work in tempera focusing on the negative side of the military regime; Emilio Torres (1944–?) of Panama City; Brooke Alfaro (1949–?); and David Solís (1953–?).

Raúl Vásquez (1954–?), who is from Los Santos, influenced several painters from that area, including Roosevelt Díaz Herrera (1963–?), who would go on to be part of an unofficial group referred to as *La Escuela de Azuero* (the Azuero School).

Female Artists

The artistic world in Panama has also had its share of female artists who made a name for themselves; among the most recognizable are Trixie Briceño (1911–1985), Olga Sánchez (1921–?), Coqui Calderón (1937–?), Teresa Icaza (1940–?), Olga Sinclair (1957–?), and Isabel de Obaldía (1957–?).

Trixie Briceño is among a handful of Panamanian painters who use animals, especially cats, in their work. Olga Sánchez uses the human body as a theme in her work, while Tereza Icaza is known for her use of geometric structures and collages. Coqui Calderón started her art studies at the Rosemont College in Pennsylvania and later studied at the Academie de la Grande Chaumiere and the Académie Julie in Paris. Her work is clearly influenced by pop art. Olga Sinclair is the artist Alfredo Sinclair's daughter. She started her studies in painting with her father and later studied at the Escuela de Artes Aplicadas y Oficios Artísticos de Madrid in Spain. Back in Panama, she took classes in engraving at the *Taller Gráfico Panarte*. She keeps very active in the Panamanian community by giving talks and has received multiple recognitions for her work in the community. Although Isabel de Obaldía was born in Washington, DC, her parents were from Panama and France and she lives in Panama, so she is considered a Panamanian artist. She has done some outstanding painting of the human body and is best known for her decapitated masculine torsos. In addition to her painting, she is famous for her glass sculptures, which have been exhibited worldwide.

Another famous female name in the arts is Sandra Eleta (1942–?), who was born in Panama City. She created audiovisual pieces about Panama's painted buses and its Afro-Caribbean people. Sandra Eleta also studied photography at the International Center of Photography in New York. To date, her most important work has been on Portobelo.

Art in Panama Today

In the 1980s, art flourished in Panama. The local scenery was the focus. After Manuel Antonio Noriega was removed from Panama, many artists turned their art to depict Panama's day-to-day life, the devastation of the invasion of the country by the Americans, and, of course, the Panama Canal. Upon reaching its one hundred years of independence, Panama experienced a surge in art associated with that theme. Contemporary painters and movements are difficult to assess, as in trying to do so one runs the risk of being subjective. Today, Panama has a healthy number of established and emerging artists.

Paintings by Panamanian artist are available for purchase by the general public, in addition to the public art painting displays, some artists and independent salespeople also sell their work on the streets. It is not uncommon to see both framed and unframed art for sale at various outdoor locations, especially in the capital city or in one of the major art galleries in the country. Today, many of Panamas' leading artists also sell their art at galleries and at auctions both live and on the Internet.

Sculpture in Panama

Another form of art that is also visible throughout Panama is sculpture. Sculptures from the early 1900s are still displayed in Panama's major parks and plazas; however, most were created by foreign artists.

Although painting was the predominant art in Panama at the time of its independence from Colombia, several of Panama's best-known artists also explored the art of sculpting. In addition to painting, both Carlos Arboleda and Mario Calvit were also sculptors and instrumental in the development of the art of sculpting in Panama.

The art of sculpting by Panamanians is considered to have started with Carlos Arboleda, who studied at the Accademia delle Belle Arti in Florence, Italy, and the Real Academia Catalana de Bellas Artes de San Jorge in Barcelona, Spain. His creations are considered to be among the first sculptures of any value by a Panamanian artist. He was instrumental in the development of the art of sculpting in Panama, not only because he was the first professor of sculpture at the famous Escuela Nacional de Artes Plásticas in the early 1960s, but also because he founded the Casa de Escultura in 1964 for the promotion of the arts. Carlos Arboleda has won several prizes for his work both in and outside Panama. His work is displayed throughout the republic. Among his most important pieces in Panama are a monument to Dr. Jaime de la Guardia at the San Fernando Hospital (1974), a monument to Manuel F. Zarate in Guararé (1975), a monument to Dr. Rafael Estévez in Aguadulce (1978), a bust of Eduardo Vallarino in Bethania (1983), a monument of Dr. Harmodio Arias in Penonomé, and a monument to Sara Sotillo in the Majisterio Panameño Unido.

Mario Calvit (1933–?) was both a painter and a sculptor. He was very active in the arts at the national level; he was director of the Artes Plasticas department of the Panama's National Institute of Culture. Also a book illustrator, he is best known for his three-dimensional works. His welding works are considered among the few of any outstanding value in Panama.

Another artist worth mentioning is Rubén Arboleda, who studied sculpting in Costa Rica and specialized in wood and stone carving. His work is also on display in various parts of Panama. Among his most important pieces is a carved wooden medallion for Panama's Caja del Seguro Social.

Guillermo Mora Noli (1923–1981) started his studies in painting with Humberto Ivaldi and was later able to study at the Art Students League in New York City and Chicago's Art Institute. His work in wood and stone has been admired.

Another influential figure in the field of sculpting is Ricardo Martínez, who studied under Alboleda and, in 1980, founded GANEXA, the Academia de

Bellas Artes. Other Panamanian sculptors are Carlos Enrique Vásquez, Susie Arias, Robinson Salado, Oswaldo Hernández, and Efraín Rodríguez.

The work of Carlos Alboleda, as well as that of other Panamanian sculptors, can be found on display all over the country, yet these sculptors still continue to struggle to be recognized as artists. One of the major challenges they face is that major projects are still being contracted out to international artists, and many national artists do not feel that they are considered for major projects, which helps to explain the talent drain.

Photography

When it comes to photography as an art, many of Panamas' most outstanding photographers have come from the Los Santos Province. Justo Pardo Villaláz (1938) studied art and photography at the Escuela Nacional de Artes Plásticas and has been very active in Panama's artistic life. His photographs have been on display in Europe as well as in Panama. He has won several national competitions for his work.

The *Museo de Arte Contemporáneo* (Contemporary Museum of Art), which was founded in 1962 as the Instituto Panameño de Arte (Panamanian Institute of Art), is the most important venue for Panamanian artist to display their work. The Museo de Arte Contemporáneo is a nonprofit organization that houses a permanent collection and also provides painting, photography, and sculpture exhibits of local and international artists on a rotating basis, giving Panamanian artists exposure. Another key organization for artists is the Instituto Nacional de Cultura (National Institute of Culture), which was founded in 1974, allowing young artists to display their work.

PERFORMING ARTS

Music and Dance

Music and dance are important parts of life in Panama. The enthusiasm displayed by Panamanians is especially visible and audible during the Carnival season. Loud music is a constant part of everyday life. Rhythms come from buses, stores, street vendors, and boom boxes. Like many big cities in the world, Panama City also has venues for classical music. There is a national symphony orchestra and a national school of music.

Panamanians enjoy a vast array of music. Salsa and merengue, reggae, and calypso are as popular as R&B and hip-hop. Because of Panama's geographic location, the exposure to calypso, Cuban guayanco, guaracha, foxtrot, porro, son, and quadrille are rich parts of the musical heritage present in the country. In addition to the different kinds of music, Panamanians have developed their own unique style of music and dance and have also helped create styles that have influenced music on an international scale. Panama's traditional music, mejorana, punto, cumbia, and tamborito, are now part of popular music, often competing for radio time and selling CDs.

Like the *pollera* and *molas*, Panamanian folkloric music is very much a part of contemporary Panama; there are radio stations that exclusively play this type of music. Panamanian folkloric music is not limited to patriotic or official events—some interpreters of these traditional rhythms have become local and international celebrities. Two of the most popular are Sammy and Sandra Sandoval, who interpret rhythms known as *cumbia*, and Osvaldo Ayala, who plays the accordion.

The *tamborito* (little drummer), which is a couple's dance, is Panama's national dance, and it is the most important folkloric music. The tamborito music consists of drums, a female lead singer with a chorus who, along with the spectators, clap their hands to the beat as dancers dance in a circle. Dancers wear the traditional *pollera* and *montuno* for this dance.

The *tamborito* has its origins in the music played in Europe that was transformed once it got to Panama. Panama's most famous tamborito is *El tambor de la alegría* (the Drum of Happiness). It was written in 1918 by Juan Pastor Paredes and put to music by Carmen Lagnón. In addition, the *tamborera*, which was created by Ricardo Fábrega, is extremely popular. The most famous is "Guararé."

Another traditional dance is the *mejorana*. For this dance, the singers are men and the accompanying instrument is a violin or an instrument similar to a guitar. Dancers face each other in rows. The *mejorana* is also the name for a five-string instrument similar to a guitar used in Panamanian traditional music. In Panama, there is also an annual celebration called the National Mejorana Festival.

One of the most prestigious musical celebrations in the country is *El Festival Anual de la Tamborera Ricardo Fábrega* (The Annual Ricardo Fábrega Tamborera Festival). Celebrated annually, the best composers and singers in the country participate in this festival.

The *Baile Congo* is considered a traditional form of dance in Panama. Its birthplace is Portobelo, and it is associated with *Costa Arriba*, which are communities in the northern coast of the country. The *Baile Congo* is generally performed during Carnival celebrations, special holidays, and festivals. The *Baile Congo* was created during colonial times by African slaves and their descendants. People of African descent danced to the beat of African drums, shouting, chanting, and singing in a special dialect while acting out scenes of struggles of slavery. Because Spaniards did not understand what they were saying as they where singing, they did not realize that they were being ridiculed.

Congo women dance to the rhythm of the drums, moving their hips and shaking their bodies. When men participate, they pretend to capture the women; the women are always able to escape, and that is how the dance ends. Women wear bright color dresses, while men wear old clothes with ropes around their waists with objects hanging from the ropes. Their faces are usually painted in bright colors. The *Baile Congo* is a perfect example of how Panamanian-African roots have survived.

Panama's Native Indians also have their traditional dances to celebrate different events, but these are generally performed at private ceremonies or for tourists. Generally, when performed for tourists, these ceremonies provide some economic benefit for this group of citizens.

In addition to salsa and meringue, other Caribbean rhythms also prospered in Panama. Calypso, one of the most important dances, was introduced to Panama by West Indians who came to the isthmus for the construction of the railways and the Canal. In Panama, the Spanish version of the English calypso also became very popular. At the end of the 1970s, Pedrito Altamiranda produced his version of a Spanish interpretation of calypso and eventually managed to bring together some of the most outstanding Panamanian interpreters of this rhythm. Altamiranda recorded the song *Carnaval en la Central*, which became an instant hit in the 1980s. His rhythm has lasted over two decades; even today they are heard during the Carnival season.

In the early 1980s, reggae in Spanish became popular in Panama, and as a result many new artists emerged; among them were Aldo Ranks, Cocoman, Kafu Banton, Renato, and Nando Boom, to name a few. Nevertheless, the most famous Panamanian interpreter of reggae was Edgardo A. Franco, known as "El General." Not only did El General become one of the most celebrated Panamanian artists of all times, but he has also been credited with having laid the foundation for today's *Reggaeton*. In addition, in recent years, rock groups have also become popular in Panama. Among the most popular are Filtro Medusa, Lemmiwinks, Los Rabanes, Los 33, Os Almirantes, Roba Morena, and Señor Loop.

For the last five years, Panama has had an annual Jazz Festival featuring top international jazz artists. In 2004, Panamanian pianist and composer Danilo Perez organized the first Jazz Festival of this kind in Panama. It has grown and receives the support of a number of prominent businesses, organizations, citizens and well-wishers, including the president of Panama, Martín Torrijos.

There is also an educational dimension to the Panama Jazz Festival. Many educational institutions are invited to the festival to teach young musicians who aspire to pursue their education in this area. They are also given the opportunity to audition for admission to these institutions or for scholarships. Concerts are not limited to paying patrons; the government has open-air concerts throughout the year and on special holidays. These concerts are open to the public, and local and international artists perform to the delight of everyone in attendance.

Theater

Panama's tradition with theater dates back to its independence, when performances were not only abundant but also successful, mainly because they attracted performers from worldwide. Because of Panama's key location and the relative wealth of the diverse population, performers always had an audience. Initially, performances were limited to the elite, but later they became accessible to the general public. Today, Panamanians enjoy a variety of performances and have several appropriate venues in which to enjoy them. The capital city has a number of theaters. The Anayansi Theater, the Anita Villalaz Theater, the Cúpula Theater, the En Círculo Theater, the National Theater, and the *Teatro Universitario al Aire Libre* (the Open Air University Theater) are among the most popular venues. Panama also has several theater groups, which include Abba Productions, Asociación Yorick, Fantasy Entertainment, Caleidoscopio, Cultura Escénica, Entre Amigos, Tablas, Tragaluz, Nuevo Teatro, and Verona Productions.

Panama also has an interest in classical music. In 1952, the National Orchestra of Panama was established. At this venue, Panamanians are able to listen to music from European composers. Among Panama's most outstanding composers are Santos Jorge, who wrote Panama's national anthem, and Roque Cordero, who has written prize-winning symphonies and other classical works.

Appendix A: Panama at a Glance

Official Name   Republic of Panama

Capital   Panama City

Official Language   Spanish is the official language. English is spoken by 14 percent of the population. Many Panamanians are bilingual.

Currency   *Balboa*, named for Vasco Núñez de Balboa. Although the Balboa is the official currency, the Panamanian economy has been linked to the U.S. dollar since its independence in 1903.

Territory   Panama is divided into nine provinces: Bocas de Toro, Chiriquí, Colcé, Colón, Darién, Herrera, Los Santos, Panama, and Veraguas. There are also five indigenous territories.

Size   30,193 miles square (78,200 square kilometers). Of the 30,193 square miles, about 600 square miles of land are islands lying off the mainland. The narrowest part of the isthmus is 30 miles across.

Highest Peak   11,401 feet in altitude (3,475 meters). Barú (inactive volcano), in Chiriquí province.

Climate   Tropical climate with constant high temperatures. Dry period from January to April. Greater rainfall occurs in the north of the country.

Population   July 2008 (estimate): 3,09,679 people.

Literacy   Males 92.5 percent and females 91.2 percent (2000 census)

Life Expectancy   Males: 74.08 years; females: 79.81 years (2008)

GDP—per capita $10,300 (2007)

Religion   Roman Catholic 85 percent, Protestant 15 percent

National Flower   *Flor del Espíritu Santo*

National Tree   Panama Tree

National Bird   *Aguila Arpa*

Appendix B: Presidents/Leaders of Panama 1904–2005

MEMBERS OF THE PROVISIONAL GOVERNMENT JUNTA, 1903–1904

José Agustín Arango: November 3, 1903–February 20, 1904
Tomás Arias: November 3, 1903–February 20, 1904
Federico Boyd: November 3, 1903–February 20, 1904

PRESIDENTS OF PANAMA, 1904–PRESENT

Manuel Amador Guerrero: February 20, 1904–October 1, 1908
José Domingo de Obaldía: October 1, 1908–March 1, 1910
Carlos Antonio Mendoza (acting): March 1, 1910–October 1, 1910
Federico Boyd (acting): October 1, 1910–October 5, 1910
Pablo Arosemena Alba (acting): October 5, 1910–October 1, 1912
Belisario Porras Barahona: October 1, 1912–October 1, 1916
Ramón Maximiliano Valdés: October 1, 1916–June 3, 1918
Ciro Luis Urriola (acting): June 3, 1918–October 1, 1918
Pedro Antonio Díaz (acting): October 1, 1918–October 12, 1918
Belisario Porras Barahona: October 12, 1918– January 30, 1920
Ernesto Tisdel Lefevre (acting): January 30, 1920–October 1, 1920
Belisario Porras Barahona: October 1, 1920–October 1, 1924
Rodolfo Chiari: October 1, 1924–October 1, 1928
Florencio Harmodio Arosemena: October 1, 1928–January 3, 1931
Ricardo Joaquín Alfaro Jované (acting): January 16, 1931–June 5, 1932
Harmodio Arias Madrid: June 5, 1932–October 1, 1936

Juan Demóstenes Arosemena: October 1, 1936–December 16, 1939
Ezequiel Fernández Jaén (acting): December 16, 1939–December 18, 1939
Augusto Samuel Boyd (acting): December 18, 1939–October 1, 1940
Arnulfo Arias Madrid: October 1, 1940–October 9, 1941
Ricardo Adolfo de la Guardia Arango: October 9, 1941–June 15, 1945
Enrique Adolfo Jiménez Brin (provisional): June 15, 1945–August 7, 1948
Domingo Díaz Arosemena: August 7, 1948–July 28, 1949
Daniel Chanis Pinzón: July 28, 1949–November 20, 1949
Roberto Francisco Chiari Remón: November 20, 1949–November 24, 1949
Arnulfo Arias Madrid: November 24, 1949–May 9, 1951
Alcibíades Arosemena: May 9, 1951–October 1, 1952
José Antonio Remón Cantera: October 1, 1952–January 2, 1955
José Ramón Guizado Valdés: January 2, 1955–March 29, 1955
Ricardo Arias Espinosa: March 29, 1955– October 1, 1956
Ernesto de la Guardia Navarro: October 1, 1956–October 1, 1960
Roberto Francisco Chiari Remón: October 1, 1960–October 1, 1964
Marco Aurelio Robles Méndez: October 1, 1964–October 1, 1968
Arnulfo Arias Madrid: October 1, 1968–October 11, 1968
José María Pinilla Fábrega (Chairman Provisional Junta): October 12,
    1968–December 19, 1969
Demetrio Lakas Bahas: December 19, 1969–October 11, 1978
Aristides Royo: October 11, 1978–July 31, 1982
Ricardo de la Espriella: July 31, 1982–February 13, 1984
Jorge Illueca: February 13, 1984–October 11, 1984
Nicolás Ardito Barletta Vallarino: October 11, 1984–September 28, 1985
Eric Arturo Delvalle: September 28, 1985–February 26, 1988
Manuel Solís Palma (acting): February 26, 1988–September 1, 1989
Francisco Rodríguez (provisional): September 1, 1989–December 20, 1989
Guillermo Endara: December 20, 1989–September 1, 1994
Ernesto Pérez Balladares: September 1, 1994–September 1, 1999
Mireya Moscoso: September 1, 1999–September 1, 2004
Martín Torrijos: September 1, 2004–

Appendix C: Important Military Leaders, 1968–1989

PROVISIONAL GOVERNMENT OF COLONELS (JUNTA)

Colonel José María Pinilla/Colonel Bolívar Urrutia: October 11, 1968–
    December 18, 1969
Colonel Boris Martínez: October 11, 1968–February 24, 1969
Brigadier General Omar Torrijos Herrera (formerly a colonel): October 11,
    1968–August 1, 1981
General Florencio Flores: August 2, 1981–May 3, 1982
General Rubén Darío Paredes del Río: May 3, 1982–August 12, 1983
General Manuel Antonio Noriega: August 12, 1983–December 19, 1989

Glossary

Abrazo   Embrace, hug

Arroz blanco   White rice

Arroz con coco   Rice cooked with coconut cream

Babucha   Shoe worn with national costume

Balboa   Monetary unit, a coin equivalent to the U.S. dollar

Bollo   Corn cake/bun

Brindis   Toast

Calle abajo   Downtown street

Calle arriba   Uptown street

Cena   Dinner

Chicha   Light, refreshing drink

Chicha de maíz   Fermented corn drink

Comparsas   Groups of colorfully dressed carnival street dancers

Conquistador   Spanish conqueror of the New World

Cordillera   Mountain range

Costeño   A person of African ancestry, usually from the Atlantic coast

Cuadro de honor   Honor role

Desfile   Parade

Diablos Rojos   Buses used for public transportation colorfully decorated

Empanada de maíz   Corn turnover

Entierro   Burial

Guayabera   Popular style of shirt

Hojaldres   Fried dough made of flour

La Invasión   Term used by Panamanians to refer to Operation Just Cause

Lotería   Lottery

Licenciatura   B.A. or B.S. degree

Madrina   Godmother

Mestizo   A person of mixed ancestry

Mola   An art form of the Kuna Indians

Montuno   National costume for men (shirt)

Nacimiento   Nativity scene

Peines, peinetas   Decorative combs

Peinetones   Large hair decorations

Pollera   National dress costume for women

Primaria   Elementary school

Primer ciclo   Grades seventh through ninth

Rabibalancos   Literally means "white tail"; refers to white upper class

Querida   Mistress

Quinceañera   Celebration of a young lady's fifteenth birthday

Reggaeton   Latin rap

Segundo ciclo   Tenth through twelfth grade

Soberania   Sovereignty

Templeques   Hair decorations worn with the pollera

Velorio   Equivalent to a wake

Zona   Referring to the former Panama Canal Zone

Bibliography

Rodney D. Anderson, "Panama Canal." In *Encyclopedia of Latin America*. Ed. Helen Delpar. New York: McGraw, 1974.

Gustave Anguizola, *Phillippe Bunau-Varilla: The Man behind the Panama Canal*. Chicago: Nelson-Hall, 1980.

Joyce Bennett-Justus, "Women's Role in West Indian Society." In *The Black Woman Cross-Culturally*. Ed. Filomina Chioma Steady. Cambridge: Schenkman, 1981. 431–450.

John Biesanz and Mavis Biesanz, *The People of Panama*. New York: Columbia University Press, 1955.

George Black, *The Good Neighbor: How the United States Wrote the History of Central America and the Caribbean*. New York: Pantheon Books, 1988.

Norbert C. Brockman, *An African Biographical Dictionary. Denver: Panamá: Cien Años de República*. Comisión Universitaria del Centenario de la República. Panamá: Manfer, 2004.

Richard D. E. Burton and Fred Reno, eds., *French and West Indian: Martinique, Guadeloupe, and French Guiana Today*. Charlottesville: University Press of Virginia, 1995.

Rafael Candanedo, "Periodismo sin tembladera (cien años de periodismo en Panamá." In *Panamá: Cien Años de República*. Comisión Universitaria del Centenario de la República. Panamá: Manfer, 2004. 349–365.

R. Castillero and J. Ernesto, *Historia de Panamá*. 11a ed. Panamá: Distribuidora del Pacífico, 1995.

Michael L. Conniff, *Black Labor on a White Canal:* Panama, 1904–1981. Pittsburgh: University of Pittsburgh Press, 1985.

Michael L. Conniff and Thomas J. Davis. *Africans in the Americas*. New York: St. Martin's, 1994.

Jorge Conte-Porras and Eduardo E. Castillero L. *Historia de Panamá y sus protagonistas*. Panamá: Lewis, 1998.

Gladys B. de Ayala, Emilia R. de Ramirez, and Susan R. de Torrijos, *Panorama de las literaturas hispanoamericana y panameña*. 17a ed. Panamá: Ministerio de Educación, 1983.

Noris Correa de Sanjur, *Historia de Panamá*. San José, Costa Rica: Litografía e Imprenta LIL, 1995.

Jules Dubois, *Danger over Panama*. Coral Gables: Bobbs-Merril, 1964.

Encyclopedia of U.S. Foreign Relations. Ed. Bruce W. Jentleson and Thomas G. Paterson. 4 vols. New York: Oxford University Press, 1997.

Augusto Fábrega, *Por los senderos de la patria y más allá*. Panamá: Imprenta Universal Books, 2002.

Stephen A. Flanders and Carl N. Flanders, *Dictionary of American Foreign Affairs*. New York: Macmillan, 1993.

Focus on Panama. Vol. 31, no. 1. Panamá: Focus Publications (Int.), S.A., 2005.

Focus on Panama. Vol. 31, no. 2. Panamá: Focus Publications (Int.), S.A., 2005.

Timothy L. Gale, *Worldmark Encyclopedia of the Nations: Americas*. 9th ed. 5 vols. Detroit: Gale, 1998.

Valerie Wooding Goertzen, "Calypso." In *The World Book Encyclopedia*. Vol. 3. Chicago: World Book, 1994, 71.

Ileana Gólcher, ed., *Este País, un Canal: Encuentro de Culturas*. Panamá: CEASPA, Naciones Unidas, 1999.

Paul B. Goodwin, *Global Studies. Latin America*. 12th ed. Dubuque: McGraw-Hill/Contemporary Learning Series, 2007.

Samuel A. Gutierrez, *Arquitectura Panameña: Descripción e Historia*. Panamá: Editorial Litográfica, 1966.

Yolanda Hackshaw, "El reto de la difusión cultural en el Istmo: cien años de esfuerzos." In *Panamá: Cien Años de República*. Comisión Universitaria del Centenario de la República. Panamá: Manfer, 2004.

Basil C. Hedrick and Anne K. Hedrick, *Historical Dictionary of Panama*. Metuchen, NJ: Scarecrow, 1970.

J. Michael Hogan, *The Panama Canal in American Politics: Domestic Advocacy and the Evolution of Policy*. Carbondale: Southern Illinois University Press, 1986.

David Howarth, *Panama: Four Hundred Years of Dreams and Cruelty*. New York: McGraw, 1966.

Eric Jackson, "Saving Roberto Lewis's masterpieces." *The Panama News*. Vol. 6, no. 19. September 15–October 5, 2000. http://www.thepanamanews.com/pn/v_06/editions/articles/Arts.html.

Bruce W. Jentleson, "Roosevelt, Theodore." In *Encyclopedia of U.S. Foreign Relations*. Ed. Bruce W. Jentleson and Thomas G. Paterson. Vol. 4. New York: Oxford University Press, 1997.

Benjamin Keen, *A History of Latin America*. 4th ed. Boston: Houghton, 1992.

Monica Kupfer, "Central America." In *Latin American Art in the Twentieth Century.* Ed. Edward J. Sullivan. London: Phaidon Press, 1996.

Walter LaFerber, *The Panama Canal: The Crisis in Historical Perspective.* New York: Oxford University Press, 1978.

Thomas M. Leonard, "Monroe Doctrine." In *Encyclopedia of Latin American History and Culture.* Ed. Barbara A. Tenenbaum. 4 vols. New York: Scribner's, 1996.

John M. Lipski, *Latin American Spanish.* London: Longman, 1994.

Sheldon B. Liss, *The Canal: Aspects of the United States-Panamanian Relations.* South Bend: University of Notre Dame Press, 1967.

Edward Lucie-Smith, *Latin American Art of the 20th Century.* 2nd ed. London: Thames and Hudson Ltd., 2004.

Vera V. Martínez T. and Dennis J. Trisker, *Ellos también creen.* Costa Rica: Litografía e Imprenta LIL, S.A., 1992.

Macmillan Concise Dictionary of World History. Comp. Breuce Wetterau. New York: Macmillan, 1983.

William David McCain, *The United States and the Republic of Panama.* New York: Russell and Russell, 1965.

John Major, *Prize Possession: The United States and the Panama Canal 1903–1979.* Cambridge: Cambridge University Press, 1993.

G.A. Mellander, *The United States in Panamanian Politics: The Intriguing Formative Years.* Danville: Interstate Printers and Publishers, 1971.

Rodrigo Miró, *La literature Panameña.* Panamá: Editorial Universal, 1996.

George D. Moffette III, *The Limits of Victory: The Ratification of the Panama Canal Treaties.* Ithaca, New York: Cornell University Press, 1985.

Carlos Montúfar, "Historia de la fotografía en Panamá." In *Panamá: Cien Años de República.* Comisión Universitaria del Centenario de la República. Panamá: Manfer, 2004. 336–338.

Elsa María Morales Cordero et al. *Historia 1.* Panamá: Santillana, 1997.

Abdulkhabeer Muhammad, "A Brief History of the Muslims in Panama." http://www.islamawareness.net/LatinAmerica/panama.html.

"Panamá." *Enciclopedia hispánica.* Barcelona: Encyclopedia Britannica Publishers, 1995.

"La Pintura en Panamá (Primera Entrada)." In *Tragaluz,* Año 1, no. 3. http://www.tragaluzpanama.com/03/plastica/plastica_02p1.html.

Pedro Luis Prados, "La Pintura en Panamá, (Primera Entrada)." In *Tragaluz,* Año 1, no. 2 Junio-Julio 2006. http://www.tragaluzpanama.com/02/plastica.html.

Thomas L. Purvis, *A Dictionary of American History.* Cambridge: Blackwell, 1995.

Patricia W. Rader, "Rumba." *World Book Encyclopedia.* Vol. 16. Chicago: World Book, 1994, 519.

Ángel Revilla Argüeso, "La escultura en Panamá." In *Panamá: Cien Años de República.* Comisión Universitaria del Centenario de la República. Panamá: Manfer, 2004. 309–314.

Steve C. Ropp, *Panamanian Politics: From Guarded Nation to National Guard.* New York: Praeger, 1982.

La Verne M. Seales Soley, "Carlos Guillermo Wilson," *Africana: Encyclopedia*. New York: Perseus Publishing, 1999: 2002–2003.

La Verne M. Seales Soley, "El panameño de descendencia afro-antillana como autor y como personaje: El caso de Carlos Guillermo Cubena Wilson." In *Istmo: Revista virtual de estudios literarios y culturales centroamericanos*, no. 5 enero–junio 2003. http://www.denison.edu/collaborations/istmo/n05/articulos/panameno.html.

Lisa Shaw and Stephanie Dennison, *Pop Culture Latin America!: Media, Arts, and Lifestyle*. Santa Barbara, California: ABC-CLIO, 2005.

Jacqueline Shields, "A Brief History of the Muslims in Panama." *Jewish Virtual Library*. http://www.islamawareness.net/LatinAmerica/panama.html.

Thomas M. Stephens, *Dictionary of Latin American Racial and Ethnic Terminology*. Gainesville: University of Florida Press, 1989.

Bob Stiff, "A Toda Vela 'A lot more than tapas and fusion.'" In *The Visitor/El Visitante*. Vol. 13, no. 7. April 5, 2007. http://focuspublicationsint.com/New_Site/Visitor13-7/places_visitor.html.

Carlos Guillermo Wilson, "El aporte cultural de la etnia negra en Panamá." *Istmo: Revista virtual de estudios literarios y culturales centroamericanos*, No. 7 noviembre–diciembre 2003. http://www.denison.edu/collaborations/istmo/n07/articulos/aporte.html.

Carlos Guillermo Wilson, "The Role of the Afro-Latino Writer and the Quincentenary (1492–1992)." *Afro-Hispanic Review* 10, no. 3 (September 1991): 67–71.

Fernando Ureña Rib, "Esencia de Panamá en Manuel Chong Neto." http://www.latinartmuseum.com/chong_neto.htm.

Erik Wolfschoon, "La pintura en Panamá." In *Panamá: Cien Años de República*. Comisión Universitaria del Centenario de la República. Panamá: Manfer, 2004: 294–308.

WEB SITES

"Directorio de escritores vivos de Panamá." http://www.pa/secciones/escritores/index.html.

"Panama Country Study." http://www.country-studies.com/panama/religion.html.

"The Panama Guide." http://www.inpanamaguide.com/index.php?tag=tocumen-international-airport.

"Panama: The Society and its Environment." http://www.mongabay.com/reference/country_studies/panama/SOCIETY.html.

Index

About the Author

LA VERNE M. SEALES SOLEY is Associate Professor of Modern Languages at Canisius College in Buffalo, New York.